WHAT THE WORLD HEARS

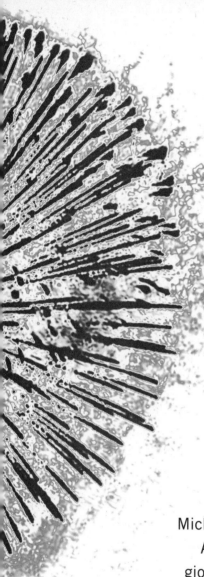

WHAT
THE
WORLD
HEARS

EDITORS
Michael McLaughlin
Alexa Mergen
giovanni singleton

CALIFORNIA POETS IN THE SCHOOLS
2009 STATEWIDE ANTHOLOGY
45th ANNIVERSARY EDITION

First printed November 2009

10 9 8 7 6 5 4 3 2 1

Manufactured in the United States of America

ISBN 0-939927-50-0

Printed by McNaughton & Gunn, Saline, MI
Typeface: Adobe Caslon Pro and Trade Gothic Medium
Cover photograph courtesy PDPhoto.org
(http://www.pdphoto.org/PictureDetail.php?mat=&pg=7568)

Alumni poems compilers: Karen Llagas and Susan Sibbet
Anthology compiler: Tina Pasquinzo
Resources editor: Amanda Chiado
Book designer and production: Francesca Pera
Copy editor: Carolyn Miller
Project coordinator: Terri Glass

To order copies of *WHAT THE WORLD HEARS*, please contact:
California Poets in the Schools
1333 Balboa Street, #3
San Francisco, CA 94118
(415) 221-4201
www.cpits.org • info@cpits.org

CONTENTS

ACKNOWLEDGMENTS

California Poets in the Schools is grateful to the hundreds of individuals, foundations, and government agencies who graciously offer their support.

ANGELS
Anonymous, Anonymous, Cathy Barber & Alan Brenner, Daryl & Phyllis Chinn, Christine Kravetz, Susan & David Sibbet, and in memory of Alison R. Bermond

BENEFACTORS
Lee Doan, Gail Entrekin, Barbara Ann Frank, Mary Lee Gowland & John Busch, Marvin Hoffenberg, Kayla Krut & Family, Nels Christianson & Flammarion Ferreria, Dave & Roma McCoy, Daniel Meisel & Amy Wendel, Mrs. Stephanie Mendel, Ruth Sherer

LEADERS
Albert Flynn DeSilver, Kathy Evans, Mr. & Mrs. A. Lee Follett, Shelby & Frederick Gans, Alison Geballe, Jane Hirshfield, Paul Hoover, Joanne Kyger, Allan Lasher, Kay Ryan, Theodore & Suzanne Seton, Anne W. Smith, Susan E. Stewart, Roselyne C. Swig, Peter B. Wiley & Valerie Barth, and in memory of Alice Gray

PATRONS
Chuck Adams, Thomas Benét, Tina Cervin, Laura & Scott Cooper, Eleanor & Francis Ford Coppola, Ruth Cox & Milton Chen, Maggie Chen, Dorothy Dumas, Rebecca Foust, Annette Bianchi & Sara Furrer, Natalie Gendler, Suzette Murphy &

Paul Hockett, Mark Lambert & Kelly Ilnicki, Daria Joseph, Raymond Lifchez, Christopher Marshall, Janice Mirikitani, Stephen Rentmeesters, Alice & William Russell-Shapiro, Robert & Joan Saffa, Shelly Sharp, Mara Sheade, Patricia Tsai

SPONSORS

Opal Palmer Adisa, Beulah Amsterdam, Karen Benke, A.S. & Jeanne Bennion, Linda Artel & Bruce Berg, Donna Levin-Bernick & Michael Bernick, Carolyn Bollinger, Maggie & Guy Calladine, Robert Carroll, Kimberly Connor, Robert Cox, Katherine & Gregg Crawford, Gordon Davies, Doris A. Davis, Betty Denton, Nancy & Dale Dougherty, Richard Dysart & Kathryn Jacobi Dysart, Victoria Ehrlich, Jane Elsdon, Sandra K. Erickson, David & Vicki Fleishhacker, Rebecca Foust, Betsy & Douglas Franco, Donna Franzblau, J. Ruth Gendler, Heather Anderson & James Craig Ghiloni, Paula Gocker, Dale & Philip Going, Nick & D'Elle Goldman, Jack Grapes, Brenda Hillman & Robert Hass, Lyn Hejinian, Torre C. Houlgate-West, Carol Kent Ireland & Uncle Don B. Fanning, Rebecca Jennings & Walter Mann, Valerie Johns, George & Sylvia Johnson, Debra Johnson, Barbara Jourdonnais, Dan Bellm & Yoel Kahn, Jane Kaplan & Donatello Bonato, Paul & Joanne Kelly, Heidi Kepper, Gerrett Snedaker & Diane Krause, Dorothy Kravetz, Eric & Katharine Kravetz, Jacqueline Kudler, Lynne Lane, Lucia Lemieux, Lynn & David Loux, Helen S. & Leon J. Luey, Joan Marler, Robert McLaughlin, Diane Moore, Abigail Ocobock, Felicia Oldfather, Ruth Palmer, Candace Pemberton, Ira & Edith Plotinsky, Neal Powers, Lynne Rappaport, Jim Rees, Eleanor Reich, Barbara & Nigel Renton, Sheila Campbell & Woody Reynolds, Connie Mobley-Ritter & Charles Ritter, Ivy & Leigh Robinson, Susan & Andre Roegiers, Elizabeth Rosenberg, Susie Schlesinger, Ruth & Alan Scott, Margo Seltzer, Emily Carlson & Phil Sibbet, Murray Silverstein, Gerrett Snedaker, Adam Somers, Jan Woodward Stevenson,

Gretchen & Grover Stone, Jean-Louise Thacher, Andrea
& Richard Triolo, Karen Cross Whyte, Steven Wright, Jan
Young

GOVERNMENT, FOUNDATION, & CORPORATE SUPPORTERS

The Association of Writers & Writing Programs (AWP),
Barnes & Noble, Books Inc., California Arts Council, City
of San Buenaventura, Community Foundation of Sonoma
County, Community Thrift Store, The Companion Group,
The Richard F. Dwyer – Eleanor W. Dwyer Fund, Entrekin
Family Foundation, eScrip, The Frank Foundation, The
Grove Consultants International, Walter & Elise Haas Fund,
The Heartlink Network of Point Loma, Marin Community
Foundation, Dave & Roma McCoy Family Foundation,
National Endowment for the Arts, PEN Center USA,
Poetry Flash, Poets & Writers, Sher-Right Fund, Sidney
Stern Memorial Trust, Theatre Bay Area, Zellerbach Family
Foundation
And the arts councils of Alameda, Humboldt, Lake, Madera,
Marin, Mendocino, Sacramento, San Diego, Santa Barbara,
San Luis Obispo, and Sonoma Counties

FOREWORD

Looking Back, Looking Forward

A couple of weeks ago my neighbor Sam came to help me with a computer issue. He's fifteen, taller than me, and polite enough to take off his grass-stained shoes at the front door and help this old guy out. You see, I'm an OG (Old Guard) on the basketball court, and Sam wants to know the secret of my hook shot. We've played one-on-one for years, since he came up only to my chest and could hardly dribble without bouncing the ball off his shoes. He thinks that I can dispense wisdom that would improve his game with his friends. He has yet to beat me.

Before Sam started addressing my computer question (something, I'm sure, that every third-grader knows), he asked, "Hey, what's that?" "What's what?" I asked in return. He flicked his chin at my IBM Selectric typewriter and once top-of-the-line machinery, the mainstay of every poet or writer.

"You mean the typewriter?" I asked.

Sam looked at it, a smile building up on his smirking face. "Oh, so that's what they look like."

Immediately I felt like Fred Flintstone. I almost said as much but I was scared that maybe Sam wouldn't know Fred Flintstone and his signature "Yabba-Dabba-Doo!" So I demonstrated the keyboard action, each letter exploding black ink on white paper. Sam smirked some more and remarked, "It's loud."

I had to chuckle as I turned off the typewriter humming like a refrigerator. I asked Sam to solve my computer problem — solve it but don't bother telling me how you did it.

He did his task in a matter of minutes, sighing noticeably because my problem was, like, so obvious. I rewarded him with cookies and sent him away with crumbs falling from his lips.

But I love my typewriter, an object now for museums. When I first became a poet in 1973, a student at Fresno City College, I wrote my poems in longhand. It was the way poetry was made, and perhaps how it's still made today. This is what I would ask the young poets in this anthology: How do you write yours — in longhand in pencil, or by computer? If you're in love, do you write lines in the sand and let the waves eat away at your creation? (Intense love, they say, is ephemeral.) Poetry is written for our own record — after all, we can't remember everything. We need a device to make it permanent! Most know that at one time poetry was learned by heart. You recited it until it was part of you.

Now we have permanence in the form of this anthology — it celebrates the poetry of young people and the milestone forty-fifth anniversary of California Poets in the Schools. Do more than thumb through these pages. Read them all. I'm thinking right now of the lines conjured up by fourth-grader Auggie Buschman, who ends his poem with, "The Alaskan language / at the bottom / is waiting to / rise." First, let me tell you that in Auggie's poem "the bottom" is the ocean; second, these lines imply that the native language of Alaska will resurface and become speech; third, the poem has such a confidence — yes, the native language will become renewed, he's certain of it; fourth, that we will tire of our own language and wait for something more spiritually nourishing.

What I'm doing here is a close reading of Auggie's poem,

playing around with ways of reading it, sort of exercising my imagination. I'm seeing what a fourth-grader is seeing, and it is providing this OG delight — I'm smiling at this moment. He's tapped his heart and imagination and fed his creation into my own heart and imagination. In short, he's sharing.

This anthology is filled with such poems. In "mini poems" by fifth-grader Gavin Sakamoto, I'm thrilled by this haiku-like image: "fire: / the killer / fist of hell." Here I don't have so much a smile on my face as I do surprise. How did he come up that? Why didn't I think of it first? Gavin also writes: "popular: / not forgotten / in a group." Ah, a new way of thinking of popularity at school. Or, just think of the single line by eighth-grader Alanna White, who in "Best Friends," says: "The lawyers prosecute my tears and win." Here again we have heart and imagination, and this line has this OG of a poet thinking, ""Now why didn't I do that first! It's not fair!"

But no crocodile tears from this poet — no way! I'm in awe of these young poets. It rekindles my own poetic energy. Perhaps I will write a poem today, certainly tomorrow. I will write old school — first in longhand on lined yellow paper, then copied by typewriter. The keys will explode on the paper, like fireworks, I pray. Let me provide a little light, no matter how temporary.

Now back to my neighbor Sam. He has come and gone, and will come again, I'm sure. In time, he will be not only much taller than I but also on his own. He'll have solved that hook-shot for the simple act of trying. We can say the same for the young poets in this anthology. They'll return and return to poetry, and although they will never solve its trickery (no poet ever does), they will have participated, wonderfully so, in the oldest literary expression known to humankind.

Gary Soto

LETTER FROM THE CODIRECTORS

Dear Friends:

This anthology marks the forty-fifth anniversary of California Poets in the Schools, one of the oldest and the largest writers-in-residence programs in the country, each year bringing poetry and creative writing to over twenty-eight thousand California students. Our annual anthology of student poems, poet-teacher poems, essays, and lesson plans has been a hallmark of the CPITS program for decades.

Because of our anniversary, this year we wanted to create a different type of anthology, one with as much emphasis on the poems of our incredible poet-teachers as on the marvelous student work that has always made up the bulk of the collections. CPITS has a two-fold mission:

1) helping students throughout California recognize and celebrate their own creativity, intuition, and intellectual curiosity through the creative writing process, and

2) providing students with a multicultural community of trained, published poets who bring their experience and love for their craft into the classroom.

In this celebratory collection, you will find both aspects of our mission illustrated through poetry. Eighty of our 101 active poet-teachers and a few alumni poets from earlier years are represented here. Add in eighty student poems written in CPITS writing workshops chosen from hundreds of submissions from all across the state, Humboldt to San Diego, the coast to the eastern Sierra. Enjoy.

We also wish to express our deep gratitude to our editorial team, giovanni singleton, Michael McLaughlin, and Alexa Mergen, who worked well together, made tough choices, and distilled the magic you hold here; Karen Llagas, who helped choose alumni poems; Amanda Chiado, who created the resource directory; Terri Glass who kept us on task, on schedule, and out of the weeds; Tina Pasquinzo, who collected all the poems and release forms, not easy things to do; and Francesca Pera, our in-house book designer, who took on quite a task and did a great job.

Cathy Barber
Susan Sibbet

EDITORS' PREFACE

With this anthology, California Poets in the Schools celebrates forty-five years of success and inaugurates a new model for editing the annual collection: three editors working as one. Through the miracle of modern technology, we were able to corral more than four hundred poems, consider them in a crossfire of e-mail, and bring together a manuscript that show-cases our artist-in-residence program.

We are grateful to the thousands of students who partici-pated in CPITS programs in 2008/2009 and, especially, those who submitted their poems, their classroom teachers, the poet-teachers themselves, the CPITS staff, and the innumerable others who lent their support.

No one will ever pinpoint the wellspring of a single poem. We do know what happens when the source is tapped: we are at one with the work, whether in its entirety or in a single line.

We also know from quantum physics that inseparable webs of relationship connect all that exists in the universe. Poetry reveals this interconnectedness in the most surprising ways. As you read these poems, may they inspire you to share poems with old friends and new.

Michael McLaughlin
Alexa Mergen
giovanni singleton

WHAT THE WORLD HEARS

A spider hears the *whoosh* of himself making his web.
My dog lies next to my bed at night and hears
my blood flowing.
I hear an ant marching.
An ocean hears the sweet song of a whale.
A squirrel hears the sound of a tree growing.
The wind hears the *flish* of a falcon diving.
A cricket hears the shrill voice of grass talking.
The grass hears the sound *groop* of a grasshopper jumping.
A bird hears the grumbling of clouds having an argument.
A tree hears the steady *thump* of an elephant walking.
The wind hears the *hic* of a cloud hiccupping.
If you listen closely
you can hear many beautiful sounds.

Owen Waite, third grade
Oak Manor School, Marin County
Erika Smith, classroom teacher
Prartho Sereno, poet–teacher

LANDSCAPE OF A CHILDHOOD

I could have stayed home
like my more industrious
brothers, Mike and John.

One learned to cut wood
in a straight line. The other
practiced piano scales.

I could have stayed home
and studied arithmetic or
read *Robinson Crusoe*.

Perhaps, it was my mother's
fault for calling me
her Rip Van Winkle.

In late autumn, I'd walk
cornfields and along
the edges of beaver ponds.

Eventually, I'd find myself
sitting and watching snow fall
as I breathed the last of autumn.

Joseph D. Milosch, poet–teacher

MY HEART IS A MEXICAN HERITAGE

Sometimes it is loud like a drumstick
banging the drum at midnight
I can celebrate many wonderful things and
traditions
I can remember memories since I was
a baby and birds started chirping like
a broken record

My heart is a Mexican heritage

When I am happy the sky turns
into a Mexican flag
There are many magical things in Mexico
like parties and celebrations with music
as loud as a tractor
There are farms with roosters, cows, horses,
ducks, chickens, dogs, pigs as crazy as ever
I can never get tired of my
cousins playing and screaming

My heart is a Mexican heritage

When my heart is upset my pet squirrel
and monkey from Mexico try to cheer me up
When I am in a normal mood,
it is a mystery
When my heart is crazy and awesome
Chargers win the football game.

My heart is a Mexican heritage
My heart is full of music at celebrations
My heart is full of sports like crazy

But most of all I love my family more than anything.

My heart is a Mexican heritage.

Tony Vega, fourth grade
Aliso School, Santa Barbara County
Rusty Ito, classroom teacher
Perie Longo, poet–teacher

FULL CIRCLE

The only path for us to take is unity

The only wide river to cross is purpose

The only genius to express is creativity

The only vesper to whisper is gratitude

The only lesson to learn is faith

The only path for us to take is unity.

Johnnierenee Nelson, poet–teacher

HALF-FALLEN SNOW

As the seasons all change then so do the leaves. From red then to green to whoever believes. To the heat of summer, to the frost of snow. Out there I will be, Oh, out there I will go.

I don't
care if

       they're
       white, I
       don't care

           if
           they're
           green

I don't
care if

       they bite
       Or are

           in
           pictures
           I've seen

           For when I get
           in my boat, Oh, I don't
           care where I row.
           Oh, my . . . don't you
           see
           you've
           read
           right
           through
           half-
           fallen
           snow!

Guiseppe Salazar, sixth grade
Taylor Street School, Sacramento County
Bob Crongeyer, classroom teacher
Alexa Mergen, poet-teacher

I HEAR BEATS

I hear beats through the ground.
Everything is gray with no color.
No people, no nothing, all alone
by myself. I have nothing to do.
I hear the wind howling in the dark.
I touch the walls so plain and smooth.
I smell smoke going through the chimney.
I see the dark clouds gathered around me.
I'm invisible everywhere I go.

Kiara Pomsyda, fourth grade
Meadowview Elementary School, Sonoma County
Ms. Duvall, classroom teacher
Arthur Dawson, poet-teacher

UNCLE LARRY'S RED COUCH

Hey, so he left.
So what? Uncle Larry always leaves.
He don't like this summer-afternoon chit-chat.
That's what it is. Don't worry about him.
He'll be back again next Sunday
Just like always . . .
Chewing on that cigar.
Right now he's locked up in his house
With the mosquitoes
Sitting on that red couch in his underwear
Watchin' Westerns,
Scratchin'.

PJ Flowers, poet–teacher

POETRY IS

Poetry is like the rain of language
It envelops us in a shawl of thought
It lures us into a world of imagination
It flows around us like a river of sun
A simple stanza can banish all darkness

A poem is like the music of nature
like a flute playing at twilight
penetrating the darkness
bringing life to the shadows
cast by a slanting sun

A poet is like someone telling a story
but in a language with concealed meaning
and where every word has importance
and its own meaning
and with each poem a poet writes
they can change the world

Charlie Kapsiak, sixth grade
Montera Middle School, San Mateo County
Ms. Volkmann, classroom teacher
Gail Newman, poet-teacher

MAN OVERBOARD

Today, my tongue, an actor
in the drama of language
has taken flight and
walked offstage.
Where he has gone and
where I should search
for him I do not know.
An old dog, my tongue
used to roll himself
asleep beside my teeth
as I slept, and when I woke,
he would fly beside the canyon walls
of my cheeks, calling out his wisdom.
Without my tongue, I can only
guess at the taste of an apple.
When I kiss you, he is missing
as I reach to touch
the tip of your tongue.
I have given him tart
and sharp cheeses, asked him to
sing a song of delight.
Someone must have stolen him.
I hear him calling out
for me to come, but
I am unable to reply and ask
him to be my guide.
And so I stumble back and forth
and hope he will know
me by touch. Were it someone
else's tongue instead,
would I understand him
by his mouth feel?
How awkward I would feel
telling someone else's truths,
someone else's lies.

Scott Reid, poet-teacher

BALTIMORE

I walked the streets
of East Baltimore
and got tired
of stepping over glass
and abandoned toy cars
at Greenmount and North Avenue
with Cisco Kids
and low riders,
avenues of yellow lines
lake trout and grease
pay phones and a lot of jaywalkers.

Baby dark shadows of summer.
The beautiful black-skinned
young brothers in their Adidas
dancing with police
and horse-drawn hearses.
The V-103 music power sweep.
The geography of sound
gospel music and Druid Hill Park
East Coast hip-hop
below the Mason-Dixon line.

Mounted police and
beer-bellied white men
clip-clopping through Memorial Stadium.
Rah-rah sirens
bells, buses, horns,
walking up steps, high curbs
and down cobblestones.

I'll not leave
the five-year-old
future teenage mothers
with their hands on their hips

shaking their tail feathers
in the face of a teenage
mutant future black man.

Down from Philly
up from D.C.
now residing in B'more.
This is where I am now
in the city that breeds
and maybe reads
that geography of sound.

minerva, alumna poet-teacher
reprinted from 1994 CPITS anthology

DIFFERENT AND THE SAME

I am the one with dirty blonde hair
Like the Hawaiian sandy shore.
My eyes are the color of ripples
In the pond, but sometimes
Green like the grass on the front lawn.
My skin is the color of butterscotch.
I'm good at playing the violin.

My friend has deep dark hair
Like a crow flying through the night sky.
Her eyes are the color of coffee.
Her skin is the color of milk chocolate.
She has parents from Jordan
While my parents are from Russia.
She's good at dancing.

We are the ones who have parents
From far-away places.
We both like rice with chicken.
Together we love our families.

Elizabeth Klimov, fourth grade
Hope School, Santa Barbara County
Mrs. Talley, classroom teacher
Lois Klein, poet-teacher

TO JAZZ

This jazz thang
Muse with sound
Reasoning
Notes season time
Equals distance
Divides velocity

How dis sound?
How dat sound?
Did you hear that
Transmission?

Make missions possible
Oh Yeah!
Crusin' jucin' in fusion
BAAM bawp de wop be bawp
Vibe tells tales
Come on!

WELL!!

Minglin, hidin' dyin' and revisin'
Leaves fall from trees
Heritage goes
WAAAAY back
Plays deep!
Miles, Coltrane, Byrd & Bessie
Free Quincy
You DIG?

Yeah!

Hear we be!
Base through
High treble knows
Middle C
Learn to discern
Melodies epiphany
Dogon see
Jazz is a Sirius Mystery!

Tureeda 'ToRead ah' Mikell, (c), poet–teacher

"EACH DAY IS A LIVING GOD OF TIME"

—from the Maya, who worshiped Time

Yes, I may die in a small room, and worse,
in some pinched space of myself
where no sky enters, where fear and pain
are all, and the first gull-sound
of the infinite is mistaken
for an old refrigerator's creak.

But to knock now on the half-locked door
opening out of the petty, the pinched,
into the heart's green soil-way,
its spring-source, flame, and river:

Is it too much to ask of this seemingly
modest day, which again arrived perfectly
over our beds and houses, with time's taper
lit, gold and great, munificent,
even while melting away?

Claudia Dudley, poet-teacher

MAYA

My Dad's family is Maya.
One of our customs is
making red bean bread.
Mushcamintic
My Grandma speaks
Maya to me
and I understand it.
Mushcamintic
I learn
a lot of things
about our past.
Mushcamintic
I learn that
our past was
harsh
in the past.
Mushcamintic.

Luis Gonzalez, fifth grade
Helen Lehman Elementary School, Sonoma County
Leslie Stirnus, classroom teacher
Pamela Raphael Yezbick, poet-teacher

I DON'T WANT TO BE FOUND

I don't want you to
look for me when I
don't want to be found.

I don't want you to
look for me when I'm
gazing at the river and
hiding in hollow stumps,
when I'm high up in
madrone trees, or staring
at the ground.

I don't want you to
look for me when I'm
doing art in my room
or looking in tidepools
for starfish or my reflection.

I don't want you to
look for me when I'm
looking for butterflies
flying in the colorless mist,
or looking for diamonds in myself.

I don't want you to
look for me when I'm
trying to see if I can
hear the stars sing,
maybe even if I'm
doing something dangerous
like diving off a cliff
into the blue sparkles of the sea,
don't come look for me.

Don't even look for me
when I'm riding wild horses,
but you might find me dreaming
of everything I just wrote.

Kendall Starr Gnatowski, fourth grade
Mendocino Grammar School, Mendocino County
Deena Zarlin, classroom teacher
Karen Lewis, poet–teacher

JOY WRAPPED IN THORNS

I come from beige,
Apartment number thirteen.
I come from the empty lot,
Lupine popping up
In the desert of my childhood.

I come from the cracked pavement,
A pool filled with dirt.
I come from this lonely place.
It nursed me to life
And I kiss the joyous weeds.

I come from the apple tree
Lost in the orchard.
I come from the kitchen
And the bottles with marbles
Placed on the sill.

I come from the bamboo,
A bathtub in the garden.
I come from the blackberries
And their welcoming vines,
Joy wrapped in thorns.

I come from the pyracantha,
Eating so-called poison berries.
I come from the trampoline,
Jumping high high high
Above prickly oak leaves.

Glory McGuigan, eighth grade
REACH Creative Arts Magnet Program
Hillcrest Middle School, Sonoma County
Kelly Sporrer, classroom teacher
Gwynn O'Gara, poet–teacher

BOTTLED SMOKE

Secrets never told
kept by friends
i've known

The missing piece
i used to call
trust

Missing
       Wanting
              Gone

The lies they
told fading with
time   The emotions
i keep forcing back

The smoke takes
their mind now, i
can see them drown
in it

Missing
       Wanting
              Gone

We'll never be apart
but we'll never be
       close

Then soon i too
will be missing
Tempted by
the wrong, disgusted
by the right

Missing
       Wanting
              Gone

Madison Whitlow, eighth grade
Pacific Union School, Humboldt County
Megan Collenberg, classroom teacher
Daryl Ngee Chinn, poet–teacher

BLUES

Oh, she woke me up in the mornin'.
She said, "Get out of bed."
Oh, she woke me up in the mornin'.
She said, "Get out of bed."

And let me tell you that waking up
gets to my head.

I said, "No, no, I wanna sleep.
I wanna stay from the mornin' heat."
Oh, she woke me up in the mornin'.
She said, "Get out of bed."

And let me tell you that wakin' up
gets to my head.

Dylan Sweet, fifth grade
Willow Creek Academy, Marin County
Nathania Jacobs, classroom teacher
giovanni singleton, poet-teacher

THE NEW SEASON: A BASEBALL SESTINA

Oh boy, I can smell it in the evening, the boy
Glinting in a white uniform, still clean, the ball
Fresh in his hand, now fleeing from his hand, now
     away from him
Fleeing through even the new air
And the new grass, green
The way a new green is brighter next

To a new clay infield, next
To the boy
Leaping across the new green
Outfield where he catches the ball
Like a new boy. The air
Is not really new, but these molecules belong to him

In a way that the grass belongs to him
And the next
Swing of the bat through the new air
Belongs to the boy
With a new taste in his mouth, and the ball
Still white, not yet having met not even one green

Blade of grass is his. You put up the green
Umbrella in the stands for him,
I bring my cooler, we grip our hats, we clench our fists
     into new balls
Of baseball fury, rows of brand-new parents next
To definitely not wiser rows of parents, my boy
And your boy battling out there in early spring air

Pushing the fine-tasting air
Back and forth between themselves, across green
Sprawling fields, themselves sprawling one boy
After the next

Into the dirt, their bodies falling full out with the hymns
Of sliding, ballads of dropping the ball,

Haiku of pop-up, ball
Drops out of air
Into glove. Or in the next
Inning perhaps an entire symphony of green
And brown stains up and down every inch of him,
My boy.

It's a game of give my boy take your boy glove hat bat ball —
Yell for him, spit into the clean gleaming air
The green vowels, the white consonants, the next game.

Jennifer Swanton Brown, poet-teacher

UNTITLED

I can't think of a poem.

I can't touch a chicken.

I can't pass Ag. Biology.

I can't feel thoughts.

I can't try any more.

Anayeli Vargas, ninth grade
Willits High School, Mendocino County
Mr. Schroeder, classroom teacher
PJ Flowers, poet-teacher

THE WALL BETWEEN

We're sitting on a picnic table talking about God.
I am trying to make sense, known to unknown,
sparkle of dew on a blade of grass in the early-morning sun
that mysterious force called love that can build you up
or destroy you. Her foot slices the air back and forth,
small fingers brush stray wisps from her eyes
then fiddle with the fringes of her poncho.

At seven she's seen many pass through:
the spotted towhee that died as we pulled
into the Bird Rescue Center and buried in the oat grass
with a song; the goldfish, Orange Smoothy; Great-Grandma
Felisa, laid out in white at the front of the church; her friend
Pablo who had just turned four, who used to gaze at water
from the hose, listening for secrets no adult could decipher.

Catalpa leaves shiver in the breeze, their long
seed pods sharp as daggers. My daughter leans
against my chest, back brushing my stomach,
heart beating through the thin T-shirt, vibrating
against the edge of my ribs. *I know what God is, Mama.*
God is the wall between life and death, a wall that is
easily broken like porcelain.

For a moment everything stops, the blue jays shrieking
in the maples, the wind, my breath. Strands of her hair
weave through the air, as if her form has shifted
into shadow I cannot place my hands on.
When I look again, I can almost see the blue clay
of her body, like a bowl, solid but smooth
fragile as glass.

Claire Drucker, poet–teacher

SCHOOL

Third grade floats as high as Ms. Cavanaugh.
We are smiley, shyly, shoelaces,
highly smart.
We float to another galaxy, like a television.
School obeys, does what we
tell it to do,
comes up, starts dancing
with screamy, colorful moving pictures like a TV,
floating squeezed tightly
in a box.

Third-Graders in Room 27
Regnart Elementary School, Santa Clara County
Mary Cavanaugh, classroom teacher
Jennifer Swanton Brown, poet-teacher

WRITING IS IN MY HEART

If the sea has waves
That go on forever
I could swim like the ocean waves.
If the sky has an atmosphere,
I could fly up and touch it.
If the paper never ends,
Then I would write, write, write.
I would write what I was doing
In my past and in my future.
If you can speak to the animals
& I can hear the wind calling me,
Then I am Mother Nature,
The source of the world.
I am every tree and flower.
The sky is my body,
The rivers, my blood,
The ocean, my heart.

Ryleigh Norgrove, fourth grade
Alexander Valley School, Sonoma County
Ms. Tharpe, classroom teacher
Maureen Hurley, poet-teacher

CYCLES AND LAURELS AND CYCLES AGAIN

the day of her hospitalization
was forest green
followed me everywhere
deep green, close to black
but not black at all
like coagulated blood

a giant windup doll
now and again
she freezes
as if someone
forgot to wind her.

Florencia Milito, poet–teacher

THE BOY IN THE GRASS

A troubled boy lies in the grass.
Although the wind blows hard
he barely notices.

A house stands tall behind him,
though he has his back to it,
as if he doesn't care.

The trees around him
may not provide shade, but
his yellow wide-brimmed hat does.

I am the curious bird
on a branch nearby. Cocking my head,
I wonder — Why he is so troubled?

Less than five years of age,
his body hardly makes a crease
in the new spring grass.

Jacqui Guy, fifth grade
Spreckels Elementary School, San Diego County
Janet Weigel, classroom teacher
Seretta Martin, poet–teacher

THE WONDERS OF NATURE

Little seed, little seed,
grow up high,

grow up high
and touch the sky.

Little grass, little grass,
grow up high,

hide a doe who is
running by.

Isabel Bahamonde-Partlan, second grade
Lafayette Elementary School, San Francisco County
Ms. Sandi Berger, classroom teacher
Susan Herron Sibbet, poet-teacher

AURA FLOREALIS

for Gilbert Phelps

Flower seller and river guide
the nomad artist
moves with the season

An old canvas knapsack
carries pigments, paper, brushes
a plywood board for easel
on hikes back to favorite spots
Tuolumne, Rogue, John Day River
for painting what can be seen
from a comfortable seat
in a side canyon's deep cleft
at the turn in the river
by the swimming hole
under a canopy of trees
where whitewater moves
like a direction of light
how shadows follow sun
as contrasts, colors and shapes
scoured up from the shoal

Indoors he paints
from memory to fill
a collection of empty vases
with the thousand bouquets
he made for roadside sell
many winters ago
from huge bundles
bought in the fields
of ethnic growers in Salinas Valley
Italian roses
Japanese carnations
Chinese chrysanthemums

with paper as a palette
colors crawl
details melt
transparent washes pool
on the face of glass and petals

Aura florealis he calls it
the breath of landscape
or glow of flowers
the stored sunlight
reflecting back
a bright northern wind

Richard Newsham, poet–teacher

UN DÍA

Un día, la vida,
life, one day,
es como un río de duraznos,
a river of peaches
Cuando los corto del árbol
When I pick them from the tree
y los pruebo
and I taste them,
siento ese jugo
sabroso, dulce
I feel the juice,
delicious, sweet.
The next day
el siguiente,
like tepache, pineapple wine,
fermentado y amargo,
fermented and bitter.

Juan Pablo Raya, high school
Sonoma County
James Peterson, classroom teacher
Jabez W. Churchill, poet–teacher

PAINTED DESERT

We stand at the edge of the painted desert,
a land layered in pastel eons.
We've come from downtown Flagstaff,
one afternoon's travel
shadowed by time and hysteria,
the heat inside a pickup,
light moving across a dashboard,
the whir and click of a million buttons,
doors, tires, chains, fans, lips.
How calm it seems with only the wind
raising dust out over the pale crimson edge
and thoughts slowing now and deepening
to reveal the handshake
of heart and land.

Duane BigEagle, poet–teacher

YELLOW

The sliding of yesterday
and power of the fields.
Not the life of sadness
but the joy of wisdom.
Cracks of wind.
Not stuck inside a black box,
but the rapids in a river
with the fish all going upstream
swish swish swish.
The sparks of starlight
and the heart of the sky.
A picnic, breathing history.
The silence of the creek.

Shay Engstrom, fifth grade
Tam Valley School, Marin County
Catherine Patler, classroom teacher
Karen Benke, poet-teacher

NOTHING ADDS UP

The boy draws himself
with a bomb head,
machine gun arms,
hand grenade feet,
and a stick of dynamite
for the heart.

My goal is not to
get bent out of shape.
It is easy to forget
what the body
actually looks like.
This is the same boy
who claims he has never seen the moon
or stood near the edge of the ocean.

I wish he could touch the heart
behind the stick of dynamite,
the one he could depend on
when the world gets very dark.

Sally Doyle, poet-teacher

HAIKU

In the loneliness

maybe I can find a moon

in the darkened sky

Fanny Cameron, third grade
Montecito Union School, Santa Barbara County
Ms. Martin, classroom teacher
Lois Klein, poet–teacher

AT STONEHENGE

At Stonehenge, in the United Kingdom
the grass is a forest green
under the gray clock-like circle of rocks
that sleep like hollow doorways
under the baby blue sky.
At Stonehenge, the rocks stand
forever like stacked dominos.
People have theories about this place.
Some say this. Some say that.
But the fact is, it is a mystery.

Mike Waara-McAfee, fifth grade
Spreckels Elementary, San Diego County
Peggy Araiza, classroom teacher
Celia Sigmon, poet-teacher

RUNNING

I couldn't stop.
Faster
And faster.
I don't know how I can
Catch my breath.

Questions, so many questions
Running through me.

Slower more slowly
Calmer, I push
I push all my feelings
Into one huge question.

I slowly release all my questions
into one big sigh.

I walk to my bed
From my chair.

My mind was running.
Not me.

Grace Bolen, fifth grade
Springhill School, Contra Costa County
Rob Fisher, classroom teacher
J. Ruth Gendler, poet-teacher

MY HEART

A shy bird is in my heart
As the blue sky rounds
my shy bird, thunder
frightens the sky   Rain
hits the ground   *tik tik tik*
The stream makes a
waterfall sound   The
stream makes all the
thunder and clouds and rain
go away   and all that's
left is that bird of mine.

Jordan Kost, third grade
Pine Street School, Inyo County
Victoria Hamilton, classroom teacher
Eva Poole-Gilson, poet-teacher

BEST FRIENDS

Those nutty millionaires
Those top executives
Those fiendish managers of my heart
Lucky I am to avoid paperwork
Because my filers file so well
The lawyers prosecute my tears and win
Oh those dictionaries of my head
I never felt so happy till the
Present people unlocked my
Complicated world

Alanna White, seventh grade
The REACH Charter School
Brook Haven Middle School, Sonoma County
Leslie Lowell, classroom teacher
Gwynn O'Gara, poet–teacher

MINI POEMS

wind:
the knife
of wonder.

freedom:
the joy
of life.

fire:
the killer
fist of hell.

vacation:
joy away
from home.

poem:
the center
of all
feelings;

socks:
not flat
cushions.

popular:
not forgotten
in a group

not only
a hobby.

falling:
going down
in silence

moon:
not the ever-
lasting sun.

California:
a golden
home

echo:
not a lonely
single voice

Gavin Sakamoto, fifth grade
Tam Valley School, Marin County
Catherine Patler, classroom teacher
Karen Benke, poet-teacher

TO MY POETRY STUDENTS

— The foundation of every state is the education of its youth.

Do not assume that because I don't call you by name,
that I do not know you. For I remember all of you,
the poems you write & all your faces shining
with the first faltering words of hope.
Do not rage against the wind or lack of memory
as if the sun had risen prematurely at daybreak
painted with rosy yearning, only to find the clouds
had forgotten how to properly mourn the tragedies
of a world drowning in the vagaries of the heart.
For once I stood alone with the voices of the wind,
my own song hanging at the end of its chord,
like Munch's silent scream echoing off the canvas,
a nocturne of loneliness, an etude seeking rebirth
before I called it poetry, before it called for me.
Sleep returns lost memory in minute increments
of time swaddled in the supplication of blue solace
unburdened by prayer or the length of the road
set adrift in the traceless grasses' slow current.
To love words requires only the longevity of a mind
that is part redwood, & part bristlecone pine
& a threshold for a mouth that is part estuary,
& part river to address the worded islands of the world.
Remember to write of what is visible and seen
pay homage to the slender names rooted in oak,
lichen & moss, reed & bracken fern, lupine wolf & moon.
Treat your poems like long-lost kith and kin.
Someday when you can forgive their waywardness
they will be Diogenes' lanterns on dark, restless nights.

Maureen Hurley

DEAR READER

Dear Reader,

Have you read your new poem? It stinks like perfume. It looks ugly like a flower. In the end I liked it like I like zombies.

Brandon Estergard, fifth grade
Terrell Elementary School, Santa Clara County
Denise Rawlinson, classroom teacher
Amanda Chiado, poet–teacher

STUNNED, SITTING

Stunned, sitting, lying, standing, I'm feeling I should run, do not make that call

Stunned, freezing cold, if snow could fall it would stay on the ground forever

Stunned, the tire tracks heading off a cliff from the truck I cannot see from my selfless position

Stunned, my heart beats faster and yet I cannot feel the pain in my hands

Stunned, I want to run, I want to run, I want to run. Stolen trouble kills me

Stunned, no silence because of the fear of what will happen. It is unclear

Stunned, I started fun. I notice I'm stunned

Stunned, do not make that call

Micah Groom, tenth grade
Golden Eagle Charter School, Siskiyou County
Alana Althaus–Cressman, classroom teacher
Beth Beurkens, poet–teacher

READING "IN GOLDEN GATE PARK THAT DAY"

I printed off twenty-five copies of the poem
On ten of the copies I'd highlighted a section
for a handful of lucky readers.
Before they began,
I told them to read t-h-r-o-u-g-h the line
to the next line
not to stop when the line ended
unless it felt right.
I told them to flow their voice across
And down the page
As Ferlinghetti had done
        Indenting here as breath
                And here for space.
                        "I don't get it." One student said.
There's nothing to get, I said,
                        It's a story
                                written in his own voice
his own rhythm
        setting a scene
                showing the small details that make up our lives
                where very little happens
                        that isn't beautiful.

Christina Burress, poet-teacher

THE FIREFLY DANCE

When the last edge of golden light melts into the sea
That is when the fireflies dance
Like diamonds sewn to the velvet sky
Or the light from a sleeping wolf's eye
They skip across the evening air
Like stones on the pond thrown
Here
And
There
Dreams that dance around my head
They light up the sky, black as lead
The silent music of the night
Or the sky's luminescent kite
When the last edge of golden light melts into the sea
I see the fireflies dance
And hope they'll dance with me.

Paige Colvin, fifth grade
Hall Middle School, Larkspur
Elaine DeMartini, classroom teacher
Terri Glass, poet-teacher

I AM

I am the comfort of a fox as it catches its prey.

I am the excitement of a learning pup.

I am the breeze that ruffles in the sky.

I am the crashing cry of skis sliding on the glittering snow.

I am the splashing of the waves.

I am the four flames of light.

I am the gentle touch of nature.

I am the love between a girl and boy.

I am life.

Benjamin Miles Castel, third grade
Lincoln School, Ventura County
Martha Etchart, classroom teacher
Richard Newsham, poet–teacher

ORQUIDEA

Ya no soy
de aquí
ni de allá,
orquidea pasajera.
El campo donde yo nací,
en barbecho,
el pozo estancado,
menos a los que permanecen
inmóbiles donde se sembraron,
cardos emperrados
al viento seductor.
Vocales y labiales,
labios mas suaves
que abren y aprietan
sin vacilar.
Bocas,
canela y chocolate,
placers quizás sin nombrar,
fruto prohibido,
menos a los que dan culto
a dioses ajenos
cuya marca no la llevo
al contario de mi propio,
su mesa al ahijado
me invitaron disfrutar.
Ya no soy
ni de aquí
ni de allá.
El campo donde yo nací
pozo estancado.
Bienvenido
donde vaya,
raices al aire,
ahijado del viento seductor.

ORCHID

I'm not
from here anymore,
nor there,
a transient orchid.
The place where I was born,
fallow fields,
a stagnant well,
except to those who stayed
where they were planted,
thistles stoically opposed
to the seductive wind.
Vowels and stops
from softer lips
that part and press
without hesitation.
Mouths,
cinnamon and chocolate
that taste perhaps of pleasures
for which there are no words,
forbidden fruit,
except to those who worship other gods
whose mark I do not bear,
who, unlike my Father,
made me welcome,
a stepchild at their table.
I'm not
from here anymore,
nor there.
The place where I was born
a stagnant well.
Welcome,
wherever I may go,
roots in the air,
stepchild of the seductive wind.

Jabez W. Churchill, poet-teacher

MATKA'S GOLABKI (MOTHER'S STUFFED CABBAGES)

for Lucia Huczek, Sr.

My mother's hugs were folded
into the cabbage of her Polish ancestors.

Every Sunday, she would stand
at the kitchen counter, like her mother
and her mother before her,
wrapping ground meat
and freshly boiled white rice
       seasoned with pepper and paprika
in little green blankets,
and gently put the bundles
into a pressure cooker
for Sunday dinner.

When the cooker began to steam
she would put the regulator on,
and it would shake and dance
like a polka.

My sisters and I would
stir the thick sour cream
until it was smooth
and snowy white
waiting patiently for
the *golabki* to finish cooking.

Every Sunday, at three o'clock
My mother's love
was on the table,
Wrapping us all
in the *pierzyna*
of family.

Lucia Lemieux, poet-teacher

pierzyna = eiderdown quilt; *golabki* = stuffed cabbage

COLORS

White is shining bright tonight
It wants to be a sun bright
shining all over the world, not
the whole garden.
Will it ever dance upon the clouds?

Purple is singing loud and bold
It sometimes wants to be a
Flower that is young and just born.
Will it ever glitter upon the night sky?

Pink is sparkling upon the moon,
it glows with glory, it lands
in my heart at midnight.
Will it ever hug heaven?

Green is wet as the grassy sky
as the sunny nights so light
so bright.
Will it ever become a part of me?

All the colors around the world
get together as they go on to the
sky dreaming a dream together.

Greta Gurvitz, third grade
Lakeshore Elementary School, San Francisco County
Patricia Arian, classroom teacher
Grace Grafton, poet-teacher

INSIDE MATHEW'S HEART

My heart is full of happiness and gratitude.
My heart is a big red sun in the morning
but at night, it's a calm glowing moon.
My heart is full of doves and trees.
If I'm sad, the doves cry and the trees die.
When I regain happiness
the doves soar and the trees grow back.
My heart is like a single flower.
When I'm sad, it falls to the ground.
When I'm happy the flower stands up and sings.
My heart is a peaceful place
where there's no war or villains — just happiness.
My heart is a place where everyone is friendly
and everything is nice with a few skate parks
and a lot of basketball courts.

Mathew Flax, sixth grade
Rancho Encinitas Academy, San Diego County
Jill Moses, classroom teacher
Jill Moses, poet–teacher

TROUT, CAUGHT

I say, "I'm
Sorry,"
To the watery eye
Of the trout I've just caught.
Holding its glitter of scales
In a tightened caress,
The knot of my hand
Gentle but sure this fish
Will not flap away home;
No mirror of the wild flashing
Of the previous slippery
Splash and slap struggle
On leaving, hooked,
The stream of all
It could know.
I am sorry, and
Hiking back up
To camp's warm
cook-fire glow,
I whisper,
"Thank
You."

Teresa McNeil MacLean, poet-teacher

THE POEM

Of all the poems
in the books on the pages in the ear on the tongue
of all the poems
with their wandering pathways their minor discoveries
terrains where the footprints are everywhere
of all the poems
written rewritten rejected and cherished
only one will be remembered.
There will be a mountain in it
a tree or the feeling of a tree
a small bird singing by an open window
although none of these may be referred to specifically.
As you read it you will hear your voice, as though for the first time
singing as once you sang, laughing, crying as you used to.
There will be an ocean wave in it
early sunlight on wet leaves
the sigh of someone who has reached the other side of pain
although none of these may be referred to specifically.
And there will be elements in it that only you will recognize
and that you may not be able to elucidate.
After you have read it, the poem will linger in you.
When all the conversations are completed
when the unspoken thoughts dissolve into silence
along with the dreams the memories the aspirations
        and the passions
the poem will whisper in your ear
like the song your mother sang when you awoke alone in darkness
like the light of a star that you looked at before you forgot to look.
Somewhere in the house where you have lived since you were born
a door will open that you never knew was there
and everything you see will tell you its name

the rocks will all open like mouths
and the springs they have ached for so long to release
will ripple and sing in the sun.

Only one of the poems
will be remembered
to write it
I would give my life
over and over again.

Emmanuel Williams, poet–teacher

IT WAS JUST TOO GOOD

After "This Is Just to Say"
by William Carlos Williams

I have eaten
All the ice cream
That was in the freezer

Which you were probably saving
For dessert

It was just too good
If I didn't I would faint.

Dean Headley, second grade
Archway School, Alameda County
Barry Turner, classroom teacher
Marissa Bell Toffoli, poet–teacher

HIS SURGEON'S HANDS

Surgeons have gloved hands
covered in red juice.

Surgeons have special hands
trained to help.

Surgeons have hands that saved
my great-great-grandpa's life.

Aaron Lerner, third grade
Canyon View Elementary School, San Diego County
Sue Ann McLaughlin, classroom teacher
Seretta Martin, poet–teacher

SCREAM

Scream. Let it out
like a secret you want to share
feel the tension, feel it tear
a hole growing in your burning flesh.

Scream the anger
shaking the ocean's furious waves
feel released adrenaline rise
close your eyes, think.

Fly like a bird high in the wind
let your scream twist and turn
a merry-go-round spinning
finding its way to the start

Scream at your fears
grow courage and confidence
scare away all the reckless
love fear, don't hate, scream

Scream, let it out
hit the ground like roaring thunder
your scream is the blanket that keeps you brave
my scream is the light inside a dark cave.

Angelika Trujillo, tenth grade
Terra Nova High School, San Mateo County
Emmanuel Williams, poet–teacher

RHYTHM

Late afternoon the dog comes to my study
and rubs her softness against me
now say her eyes
(even the patient know urgency
the dreamy wake to appetite)
among the trees she greets old friends
exults in the warmth of a new hand
at home I fill her bowl

so the heart finds where we hide
among strangers or preoccupations
and tells us it is time

feed what is hungry
air what is stale
pick up pen or phone
and pronounce the words
practiced so long in silence

or lie down in the sun with the grass
neither bless nor curse
simply change

Gwynn O'Gara, poet–teacher

WYOMING CHILDHOOD

No bird could be heard
over wind in the limitless winter.
Our skin dried like the bark
on the leafless willow tree.
When tears became ice in the eyes,
we stopped trying and came inside.
Then we marked the long days
with long sighs, burrowing
into our over-heated rooms,
foreheads furrowed over books,
hunting escape from our self-made trap
while the furnace blew our hungers back.
The wind defined the word *whine*
at the windows, where once I looked
out into the eyes of a starving deer
and, startled, saw my own frozen stare.

MaryLee McNeal, poet–teacher

BEATS UNLIMITED

Inside the drumstick is *clicky-clack-clack*
Inside the drumstick is a lumberjack
Inside the drumstick is a crashing dish
Inside the drumstick is a puffer fish
Inside the drumstick is beats unlimited
Inside the drumstick is thought contributed
Inside the drumstick is a rhythm blinking
Inside the drumstick is Einstein thinking
Bippity bop bop goes beats in the womb
I'll be layin these down all the way to my tomb
Boom-boom goes the bass drum — *crash* goes the splash cymbal
Inside the drumstick is my rhythm symbol
Inside the rhythm is a swing
Inside the swing is a wing flapping
Inside the wing is a time signature
Inside the time signature is an aperature opening and closing
Inside the aperature is an image collected
Inside the image is a beat protected.

Hank Brown, tenth grade
Tamalpais High School, Marin County
Harrison Hobart, classroom teacher
Claire Blotter, poet-teacher

CAN YOU SEE IT?

Can you see global warming ending?
Can you smell the ink of a newly signed peace treaty?
Can you feel the hostility disappearing and the hospitality
    spreading?
Can you hear the mingling among people of different races?
Can you see it?

Can you see sworn enemies befriending each other?
Can you smell the spring wildflowers blooming?
Can you feel the wind moving dandelions in different
    directions?
Who knows where they'll land?
Can you hear the eagle's wings flapping?
Can you see it?

Can you see the buffalo roaming the great plains again?
Can you smell the clean air?
Can you feel the earth renewing itself?
Can you see the magic in the moon?
Can you feel dawn?
Can you hear the horse's hooves pawing the ground among
    the meadows?
Can you see the joy?

I can.

Amanda Poe, fifth grade
Pacific Community Charter School, Mendocino County
Jeff Schultz, classroom teacher
Blake More, poet-teacher

SYNCHRONIZED SWIMMING, WINTER 1981

The little sacrifices for an art
I did not love. The Saturday
practices. Unrolling the tarp
at dawn. The steam, a little whispered
lie, rising from the pool. The first

plunge, puncturing the calm
surface, the upward rush of bubbles,
an icy flowering. The shroud
of water closing in, the cold

descent. The drills:
treading water in the deep
end, arms above
our heads. Ballet Legs across
the pool. Counting, sculling,
pointed toes. The coach

who hated me alone, who clapped
and yelled "chop-chop!" Her rigid
stance, the military swing
of her ponytail. The other

girls from sturdier families
who grouped together,
the whispered lies. The laps

swum underwater, little training
drills for death. The soreness
in my arms and legs, the pain

that was supposed to make one
stronger. Admonitions against
being a quitter. The rude

traditions. The birthday toss
back into the pool

after having showered
and dressed. The coach's angry

reprimand for giving chase
as the summer girls had done
to cheerful screams. In late December,

no one wanted a game
of cat and mouse. I knew
the drill. The swing and let
go, the flight, that cruel

delivery, the icy fingers
of the water seeping underneath
my clothes. The pain

that was supposed to make
me stronger. The shroud
of water closing
in, the cold
descent.

Jackleen Holton, poet-teacher

BIG STRAWBERRY

I'm a big
sleeping
strawberry
without a stem
never awake
never acting more mature
than I really am
I am friendly
unless
you eat me

Mitchell Kespohl, eighth grade
Arena Union Middle School, Mendocino County
Tim Bibbons, classroom teacher
Blake More, poet–teacher

TREATED FOR A GHOST DISEASE

Lying still
Treated for a ghost disease

Ready to blow
this joint
Sky high
on
Dust
on

No one breathes
no one to come home
to

ghost disease
riddled with holes
shot up with aches
upon pains upon pains

dance this horror out
dance this horror to tiny particles of another realm

havoc running
havoc dancing
havoc multiplying
on an earth out of control spinning

Spirit return
Spirit come back
Spirit be born

to me
fully
Re-covered
green

Lavender Grace Kent, poet-teacher

LIFE IN NATURE

I trust in nature
That planets will stay in their orbits
That life will go unchanging
That rivers shall run unhindered
Flowers will go on blooming
Cocoons go on breaking
Trees grow unhindered
Life goes on, in balance

I have seen this
Seen blue rivers rushing by
Seen planets in the sky
Seen the pattern of life
Soft pink primroses
Green cocoons ripping open
Rough bark of old trees, or soft, new,
Life.

Esther Osborne, fifth grade
Dana Gray Elementary, Mendocino County
Barbara Stone, classroom teacher
Karen Lewis, poet-teacher

CLAIRE'S CHILD

You bury your just-formed child
under the beech tree in your front yard.
Lean over his beginnings.
Hold his fingers and he flies.

May dreams of him heal you
the way water soothes banks.
May your eyes meet, recollect, move on.

I see you in your bedroom.
Pale yellow walls.
Cream silk comforter.
Snow in distant hills
behind an exploding sky.

Bears in their dens
take your unborn child
into their dreams.
Visit you too.
A sprinkling of snow in your bed.

Pamela Raphael Yezbick, poet–teacher

MEN'S COLLEGE

It was the first mixer.
We entered through separate doors,
sluice gates across a canyon.
Guys asked girls, of course.
All the music was lonely.
No one stared.
The only way was to look,
then walk the long width
of the narrow room.
May I have this dance?

She refused. I couldn't
smile, bow or say thank-you.
There had been no lesson
for refusal from a beautiful
stranger except to turn away,

to walk back to the guys
over a chasm reeking of nameless shame.
I felt like the skin of hardened fruit, quivering.
If I looked down I knew I would fall.
I saw no future in this dark brightness.
It is still easy to pick this scab.

In Argentinean tango,
a man or a woman
looks around the room.
If he gazes at her
and she doesn't turn away
she has accepted.
The man walks over.

They walk onto the floor.
If she raises her left arm high,
he takes her close into his arms,

but it could mean anything.
She can look at his chest
or stare off, as long as
she follows. They are done
only when she says thank-you.

Tonight I missed
your call from Miami,
our fixed gaze across the miles,
the voice I loved, love.

When we tango
your heeled feet angle
between my legs,
your ankle slides
down my thigh.
I don't want to
spoil things by looking.
It's your show.
We know how far this will go.
Please, no thank-you.

Daryl Ngee Chinn, poet–teacher

WHAT WON'T LEAVEN IN POEMS OF OUR OWN
(morning of the summer solstice)

Hellenistic pressure drops when
warm airplane flame
soothes data into auras.

Translation gives meaning
to sailing with height
in this vehicle (called The Body).

That said, meet me at an altitude
coined for hallways of Earth
under six different shades of dark today and listen.

We might discover the will
of adiabatic languages
that write their hair long to the thrill of an electric sea

or translate columns of flowers
into the arrogance of sunrise
before breeding domestic languages

from any development in writing
invested or entrenched
in the dreaded sound of jealousy.

O, sail with me past that (window I'd rather shut).
Let's hang out in atmospheric orchards
and coin the lavish word,

(God-given with pressure,
the first identifiable metaphor)
a free-moving seed

sent into the Winter of Feigned Imaginations.
Mesmerize that canon. Today, I dare you.

Molly Albracht Sierra, poet-teacher

CULTURE

When I tell my mother,
who wanted to go to college,
about the famous poets
I love, she is sorry
she could never give
me that, she could
never give me Culture.

Without books,
without plays,
without symphonies—
Those who know them,
Mother,
are not any kinder.

But without stories?
Without what I have
learned from my mother,
that one's hands
can heal, that the dead
are always with us.

My mother is helping
two old women die.
Her arms,
above the hands,
are bruised from the lifting.

Melissa Kwasny, alumna poet-teacher
reprinted from 1991 CPITS anthology

THE MAGIC WAND

In kindergarten, the nun ushered me
to the cloak closet during naptime,
ordered, "Stay here. Not a word until I return."
Wet wool coats stunk like death.
Black galoshes flopped in puddles.
Sure my end had come, I promised if I lived,
never to open my mouth again.

After too long, the door cracked
open. A bat-like shadow, finger to lips,
made a sound like wind.
Slipped a silky, snow-white gown over me.
Handed me a magic wand
and took me into the light,

spoke, "Children,
only raise heads from desks
when our wake-up fairy taps you on the top
of your head."

When they lifted, it was as if our souls
met in the dim. Small wonder

on becoming a poet in the schools,
I fashioned a wand
from a pizza box lid, cut out a star,
sprayed it silver, splashed it with sparkles,
tied ribbons and feathers flowing like thoughts
'round its stem. When the time came,

spoke, "Children,
only raise heads from desks
when you feel a tap on the top
of your head."

To this day pencils fly
as they wake up the lake of the page.
As promised, I don't say another word.

Perie Longo, poet–teacher

WINTER POEM

At the end of winter on a wide, busy street
a woman wrapped in scarf, hat, gloves
carries a parcel to post. She is not thinking
in Japanese, or wondering after simple beauty
like a flower. She did not drive her warm sedan;

the rain was too cool or steady or light.
The light was too steady and cool not to drench
herself in, the woman wrapped in scarf,
three layers and gloves. She rounds a corner,
wonders why the sidewalk is so narrow there

and covered in deep pink flowers, each petal
beautiful radiance, stopping the woman completely.
A hundred camellia flowers, she thinks,
scooping blossoms into her palm, her parcel
stuffed in a pocket. A thousand camellia flowers

witness winter's gaze at spring.
Around far corners, a teapot awaits ceremony,
tea leaves mute to the flowering.
She will stuff the porcelain with beauty,
drench herself in steam.

Toni Wynn, alumna poet-teacher

HAPPINESS

I am happiness.

I am a golden star in the heavens.
No matter how many ships you build
You will never reach me.
You may think you have but all is false.
Everything they say.

I have no family.
I am alone.
Happiness does not exist.

I am happiness.
That big golden star at sunset.

The first star in the sky.
The last to fade away.

I am happiness.

Logan Stoffle, eleventh grade
Del Rio High School, San Luis Obispo County
Rich Hovey, classroom teacher
Michael McLaughlin, poet-teacher

I AM

I am a planet in space,
So insignificant that I barely leave a trace,
I am a grain of sand
In a beach two miles long,
I am a bird with a broken wing
That has lost his ability to soar as high as the sky,
I am a human being
That has come across too many lies,

I am hopeful to the future that awaits me,
Not hopeful to meet the people along the road that will hate me,
I am hoping for the best
But preparing for the worst.

I am the starting point,
My future's at work.

Geovanny, eleventh grade
Providence High School, Ventura County
Lucia Lemieux, poet-teacher

TWO YEARS AFTER MY FATHER'S PASSING

Arise early and begin with simple things:
the open field across the fence;
the hill above, curved like the back
of a sleeping turtle; the first
grey-blue flicker of dawn.

Otherwise you'll miss
the way a door swings open, briefly,
between the trees, how light spills
from the other world into this one;
how it fills the earth
like fingers in a glove.

How it kisses your skin
as you stand at the window,

and moves on.

Arthur Dawson, poet-teacher

BROUGHT UP COLD-HEARTED

He's the king of the jungle,
cold-hearted and fierce.
A typhoon, a hurricane taking everything,
leaving a destroyed path.
A homie in the hood, brought up
to be fearless wit a chip on his shoulder.
Never to show emotion; don't even give a f---,
just grow colder and colder.
Came up to be a warrior,
a straight-up street soldier.
But left the world the way it started:
fearless and cold-hearted.

Ricco Gonzalez, twelfth grade
DeForest Hamilton School, Sonoma County
Patsy Truxaw, classroom teacher
Phyllis Meshulam, poet-teacher

MY ALPHABET

I want to give you
my alphabet,
every consonant and vowel,
syllable and sound,
the words that pulse
in silence,
the thoughts
beneath my eyes.

I want to give you
my exclamation points
for emphasis,
commas,
for clarity and breath,
parentheses,
for two people
surrounding something
so sacred
it can only be spoken
in a whisper.

I want to give you
my alphabet,
to reach back deep
in time,
to memory's remembering,
before my mother's voice:
ancient Hebrew, Aramaic,
cuneiform in clay.

Please take these letters,
shape them
with your hands,
read them
like Braille.
Please decipher me.

Julie Hochfeld, poet-teacher

ROCKET DANCE

When I blast off
the world catches my flames.
I push away from you
like robots from water,
babies from mashed peas.
As I burn into the atmosphere
all azure, I float
like a ping-pong ball.
The universe kicks up
its heels on my eyelids.
I am not afraid
in the mouth of the universe.
I am a shiny red gumball
and the door has been opened
for the very first time.

Amanda Chiado, poet–teacher

I COME FROM

I come from a place where abuse means love.
I come from a place where we try to make
the best out of life with what we have.
I come from a place where your parents
are allowed to be under the influence
and in & out of prison.
I come from a place where we eat Indian tacos
like they're going out of style.
I come from a place where they're killing our salmon.
I come from such a big family
that I run into people I don't know
and it turns out they're my cousins.
I come from a place where this used to be just our land.
I come from a place where going to the river
is like going to the water park.
Most of all I come from two tribes
known as the YUROK and the KARUK,
just a little past Hupa.

Angelica Aubrey, eleventh grade
Alder Grove Charter School, Humboldt County
Rachael Hernandez, homeschool teacher
Julie Hochfeld, poet–teacher

CONCRETE CAT

```
        cat                      kat
       katt                     yára
      katze                    kissa
     chatte                    pisicâ
   Siamese  Abyssinian  Persian  Manx  Lynx
   feline  companionship  soft  paws wet nose
   Button-Chaser Phoebe Pumpkin Jane Lydia
   Audrey Humphrey Fearless Fosdick Amber
   curious " ~ " companions " ~ " curious
   sleep     Ō     sleepy     Ō     sleep
   I've always loved everything about cats
      leopard  puma  tiger  panther  bobcat
       longhaired            shorthaired
        green eyes     ^ ^     blue eyes
         here kitty    | |    kitty cat
            kitty  come  to  bed
               felino gatitto
                   c a t
```

Mary Lee Gowland, poet–teacher

TIEMPOS Y JORNADAS

Mis poemas
son parte
de
la guerra

ineditos
y
a la carrera

escritos
antes
de
quedarme mudo

WORK AND TIME

My poems
are
part of
the war

unedited
and
hurried

written
before
I'm rendered
speechless

Jorge Herrera, alumnus poet-teacher
reprinted from 1989 CPITS anthology

FULL CIRCLE

Six months after her husband leaves,
without ceremony, she takes off
her wedding band of thirteen years.
She still feels it on her ring finger like a phantom limb.
The tiny diamond chips float aimlessly in the white gold filigree.
She remembers a story of a poet who threw her wedding band
into the Irish Sea, flushed and exhilarated by the drowning.
Her ring sits on her desk like an abandoned penny
flattened in an arcade for fifty cents
its value and weight now diminished by the crushing.

Like a nun who weds herself to God,
she decides to wed herself to poetry
to the way the words jump off the bridge
and into an ear or a tunnel of a heart.
She wraps herself around each word —
Words like *delicious* or *blackberry* or *divorce*.
She throws letters into a pot and chants
"with cupped hands
I bring you the soup of my childhood:
this hot liquid phosphorescent like the glitter of heavy cream
or the white of windblown snowflakes."

She serves tea with cookies that don't rhyme
and embraces each syllable like a morsel of moonlight.
She breathes in the memory of a lost green kiss
and learns to be satisfied by line breaks,
by pauses, by what is not said.
She stands by the sour plum trees
heavy and dark
rooted to the earth
and sings.

Jill Moses, poet–teacher

I AM WINTER

I am the snow within the sky
I am the scent of pumpkin pie
I am as dark as a moonless night
I am the black before the light
I am as free as a bird in the air
I am the black of dark despair
I am the rain before the snow
I am gone before you notice I go
I am winter. I fill the sky with lightning of hate
I am the ice below the skate
I am as dark as a bat in flight
I fill the sky with terror and fright
I am the lights on Christmas Eve
I am the thing in which you most believe
I am the frost and morning dew
I am winter and I'm after you
I am winter. I am the puddles beneath your feet
I am the opposite of clean and neat
I speed like a racecar over the lake
I do all this without a break
I spill my contents toward your head
And you run home to get in bed
I fill the sky with misery
I suck up all the light of glee
I am winter. I am the son of death and loss
I bring with me the rain and moss
The sunny days are all but gone
Until I leave and go move on
When that occurs the flowers grow
And over the hills, off I go
I wear the clouds like a stormy crown
And then I drop the water down
I am winter.

Graham Vert, fifth grade
Brookside School, Marin County
Laura Graham, classroom teacher
Duane BigEagle, poet–teacher

THE DIFFICULTIES

on the chalkboard words
don't make sense loose meaning unless we have
heartbeats
sentences connecting language to people
a place an action an idea
a twist
but we have family problems
personal and financial obstacles
what makes our mood and motive obscure
tiny particles of chance
any knowing that we look for
on shelves of books
and then the map
the map of the modern world
and I trace my finger
and they look at my hand
that slides across the paper colors of continents and countries
names of our journey evolution immigration relocation slavery
tribal world nomad families
my eyes my feet wander softly around
the room wondering about their words
what they cannot speak
what I do not know how to ask nor explain
their difficulties and what keeps us rolling
how our languages mean
what keeps up with us slowly what we are curious about
whatever beckons adjective and nouns and verbs
the moaning of the line and this pen
not a pen it's a screen
digitized language what keeps me from this and what nails me
to the chalkboard green and white and today
I wanted colors I wanted talent
I wanted to show them language and ideas

and context of this character
who is he what is his conflict
and what *pantheon of hybrids* does the writer intend?

I simply commented about obscurity my own confusion
my patois of meaning a perception without judgment
how you know any human experience that's not yours
polycultural intergalactic muralists —
yet these are the difficulties
my world on the map
my world in my head
and theirs I will never translate
how can I urge discussion or question
as the hint of emerging thought
simply bartered simply assumed simply practical
            but not essential
not the simple not the complexity
the message distant that our ancestors rolled behind our eyes
the longing for emptiness around their tents their stone huts
            or buildings
those cool afternoon flowers with fresh rain
where students cluster around a cement wall
others rushing with cell phones
animated lines by the coffee stand
and professors in their cubbies chatting over papers
we are hungry for words and understanding
so I offer another story an essay and a poem
            what do these mean . . .

and can you write one?

Tobey Kaplan, poet–teacher

CHOOSE

One plant in a field of others
One grain in a beach of many
One droplet in a wave

One person in a large crowd

Knowing smelling tasting touching
But never alone

Enjoying the world around us
Laughing as it turns
Smelling the sweet aroma
Of life's events
As they go

Maybe now
We choose

Our own way

Is this the way we want to go?

Alexandra Sciocchetti
Fort Bragg High School, Mendocino County
Ms. MCK, classroom teacher
Lavender Grace Kent, poet-teacher

I LIKE MY OWN POEMS

I like my own poems
best.
I quote from them
from time to time
saying, "A poet once said,"
and then follow up
with a line or two
from one of my own poems
appropriate to the event.
How those lines sing!
All that wisdom and beauty!
Why it tickles my ass
off its spine.
"Why those lines are mine!"
I say
and Jesus, what a bang
I get out of it.

I like the ideas in them,
my poems;
ideas that hit home.
They speak to me.
I mean, I understand
what the hell
the damn poet's
talking about.
"Why I've been there,
the same thing," I shot,
and Christ! What a shot it is,
a shout.
And hey,
The words!
Whew!

I can hardly stand it.
Words sure do not fail
this guy, I say.
From some world
only he knows
he bangs the bong,
but I can feel it
in the wood,
in the wood of the word,
rising to its form
in the world.
"Now you gotta be good
to do that!" I say
and damn! It just shakes
my heart,
you know?

Jack Grapes,
alumnus poet-teacher
reprinted from
If Only for a Day

RED BEANS

red potatoes
green beans
blue berries

red beans
green beans
blue berries

red greens
blue beans
green potatoes

blue beans
blue greens
blue potatoes

J. Ruth Gendler, poet–teacher

POETRY IS UNNATURAL

It's unnatural to call someone
across a ridge white and silent
who's interested
in someone else's bones
poetry is unnaturally shy
sitting in its milk of paper
like something a child has dropped
in the backyard
thirty years ago

Parched weeds their salt smell
soft motors of chickens
in the shade of their long red houses
the smooth skin
of my mother's hands
the way they were
always cool

You think if you can taste it
if you can get it back
in your mouth
if you return long enough
you will say it
for the first time
and it will be true

Katharine Harer, alumna poet–teacher
reprinted from 1987 CPITS anthology

UNEXPECTED GUEST

Pardon me,
bumblebee,
nestled in the dahlias,
did I disturb you?

Ducked out of daylight,
blanketed with dew,
tucked in purple petals,
did I disturb you?

I didn't mean to.

I only wanted
a weekend bouquet,
to brighten our table
with a floral display.

I'll go away.

The zinnias' apartments
are vacant
today.

Michele Krueger, poet-teacher

VERMONT STREET

Our home on Vermont Street —
named after a state I've never visited —
my memory of that house belongs to my mother.

Once every two or three years, she asks if I remember
the intruder or the police, have I recovered the memory
of the darkened hallway with a gas heater at one end?
Then the flames go out. On the wooden floor the weight of
someone's foot, and when the heater lights again,
the silhouette of a man.

From her place on the bed, she almost calls out,
"What are you doing home," because the shadow is
the height and build of her husband in Vegas on business.

She pretends to sleep and prays until it walks toward my room.
I don't remember the intruder or the policeman
whose gun I asked to see. I don't remember that night.
She reminds me the doors were locked from the inside,
reminds me so often that I believe I remember the keyhole.
Only a poltergeist could seep in, she knows.

Between the backyard fence and hedge one July afternoon,
lying in their shade and watching the back door on
      Vermont Street,
I hid from my parents. Who else would look for me?
They want to bring me indoors
where they believe I will be safe.
I remember the fence on Vermont Street
and learning to climb it, what some
neighbors call "trespass."

Brandon Cesmat, poet-teacher

I'M . . .

I'm an SB tongue with a form-fit sole and waterproof
    rocket-boosters
I'm long-sleeved, button-up, and strapped in Velcro
I'm the Swoosh, Jumpman, and Three Stripes.

I am "I'm Lovin' It" 's worst nightmare.
I got less giggz than the iPod Shuffle.
I'm like a brainfreeze for "little Einsteins" everywhere.
I'm the most fun you never had.
I'm one of those chocolate milks you got in a bag
    in kindergarten.
I'm not the PlayStation3 or the XBOX360. I am the
Super NES . . .

but wait, there's more

I'm an I want it, you got it kid.
I'm Dexter, you're Mandark.
You're Accel, I'm Leap Frog.

I'm the heebie jeebies you feel on that hardwood
    court.
I'm a fan of Market Mondays, but a bigger fan
    of Basketball Everydays.

I'm radio's 106.102.9
I'm half Cardinal, half Owl, and half Unicorn for now.
I'm rawer than sushi, I've got more bars than prison.
I am the Eleventh Wonder of the World . . . right after
    YouTube.com, sliced bread, and the iPhone.
That makes me like, better than The Incredible HULK
    on steroids or something.
I think I need some more bounce though.

Bryan Robinson, ninth grade
Lowell High School, San Francisco County
Bissa Zamboldi, classroom teacher
Susan Terence, poet-teacher

JACOB'S BRAKE

for my father

These are small things, really
but ones I can't forget:

banging produce cars on shiny rails
   like silvery threads in the early dark

the winding down of my father
as eighteen wheels hit dirt
   crossing the city limits
on the road to our house

my mother's sigh
   like rustled eucalyptus

my father skipping forth
   when gearing down, high to low
the air suddenly charged
   with barley and sweet sudan

and from the window
I hear him on the porch
   strip to his shorts
   shake the fields from his black hair

while my mother stands at the kitchen sink
   hands scalded heavy and red
she raises each Franciscan plate
   and slams it on the counter's edge.

There's no reason why
these pictures bloom in sleep
except to startle me awake
the past more present
   than this envelope of desert dark
his presence like a balm
   of cedar and sweet sage
while a cat's-claw moon
   from childhood dreams
twirls in the wrinkled sky.

Celia Sigmon, poet-teacher

WALKING

I walk, I walk,
I walk. In rain or shine.
I walk, I walk, I walk.
I walk in snow or hail.
I walk through screeching
sound or total silence.
I walk, I walk, I walk.

Summer Driscoll, fourth grade
Dow's Prairie School, Humboldt County
Judy Johnston, classroom teacher
Daniel Zev Levinson poet-teacher

CLOUD

I live on a cloud, misty and damp.
You don't need to bring water
because it's right there with you.
I love the feel,
the misty damp feel.
The wind blowing the cloud
which is blowing me.
The smell of the damp wet cloud.
It also comes in handy as a bed,
soft, fluffy.
You can look down and see buildings,
people, parks.
It's wonderful, the peace and quietness
up on a cloud.

Peyton Reynolds, third grade
Citrus Glen Elementary, Ventura County
Anne Wilson, classroom teacher
Shelley Savren, poet–teacher

WE HAVE IT

The dream
began before
Africans were tracked
on the coast of Ghana
and the Middle Passage and flesh for sharks.

The dream started before
1619 in upstate New York
where the first sixteen slaves
docked
way before Rosa Parks
and the Montgomery Bus Boycott.
It's not the singular
vision of one man;
it began before
we knew Mississippi
and fed her blood
for passage.

It lives in the Dozens,
The Second Line,
Pralines and Fat Tuesday
It's in the beat of the music
the rhythm of our walk
the slang of our tongues

The dream is us;
we got it from
old people's eyes
the way their fingers knuckle
and the glee and laughter
of little black children
starched and oiled for church

The dream lives
in heads held sure
of sisters
the confident bop
of brothers
we all have the dream
but Brother Martin Luther King, Jr.
gave it Voice.

Opal Palmer Adisa, alumna poet–teacher
reprinted from 1986 CPITS anthology

LIFE

Life, *la vida*
is like a mango,
sweet, *dulce,*
jugoso, juicy.
In bad times,
se echa a perder,
it goes to waste.
Life gets old,
se hace vieja,
asquerosa y negra,
black and nasty.

Alex Garcia, high school
Sonoma County
Celia Lamantia, classroom teacher
Jabez W. Churchill, poet-teacher

EMOTIONS

Hate is like an intricate candle
burning and burning away
locked in a dark room.

Love is the opposite,
flying away in open space.

Shy is small
but inside, the winds
are reeling in all directions.

Anger is red hot
burning inside, smoky.

All these things make one thing
and only one thing:
ME!

Laikh Tewari, third grade
Phillips Brooks School, San Mateo County
Ellie Seddon, classroom teacher
MaryLee McNeal, poet–teacher

BEAUTIFUL

I am a beautiful silver ring
With a delicate ruby on me
On the inner part of me
There are words
Beautiful words
Those beautiful words say
"Love Forever, Dad"

Rubi Madrid, sixth grade
Taylor Street School, Sacramento County
Bob Crongeyer, classroom teacher
Alexa Mergen, poet-teacher

MORNING POEM

This year's heavy crop is over now.
Just a few late rebels are plucked.
Stained fingers will return the helpful
white cereal bowl to its shelf.
Tomorrow's granola milk will not turn purple.
A new morning ritual will have to be found.

Only the unpicked dry blackberries
on high wild tangled branches remain.
Every year, when the season's harvest is over
a small sadness creeps its way inside.

I'll miss walking barefooted to the berries in pajamas
then reaching into the thorns for the plumpest.
I'll even miss the scratches.
I won't wear gloves —
the cuts seem like fair payment for delicious bounty.
I'll miss my lingering about —
the silent appraisal, the review of growth.
I'll miss inhaling the perfumes of berries, rose and honeysuckle —

I'll even miss my silliness, the mental quarrels I have —
work deadlines versus time spent in the garden.
"Surely, I have time to smell the flowers?"

I so appreciate the whole blackberry tangliness.
They don't beg for water or insist I feed them nitrogen or
handfuls of bonemeal.
They don't demand care, or any of my time.
They don't need anyone to fuss about them.

I admire their strong, tenacious, and resilient character.
You can cut them back, dig them up —
but, against all odds,
they come back,
faithfully luscious, every year.
Blackberries — survivors.

Michele Rivers, poet-teacher

THE SOLSTICE

If you hold still
you can feel the world slow down,
the planet's axis relax
as it tilts fully into winter.

Towhees fly more languidly
to the crowns of the pines
and the woodpecker's tapping
sounds slightly underpowered.

Rain falls reluctantly,
as if it wants to be snow — it liquors
down the walls of the Five & Dime;
haloes the late Christmas shoppers.

Everything shifts quietly
into slow motion: the slosh of unleaded
through the nozzle and the creak
of spinning dollars and gallons.

Even the squeal of brakes
as a teenaged girl looks up from fussing
with the dials on her radio
and sees the stop sign. Tonight's

moon rising over the Methodist church
takes its time. There is no rush.
The year is dark. That sweet blood
filling your own weary and generous

heart will slack off, too, dawdle
at the capillaries, glance a little longer
into the plasma's silver mirror.

Molly Fisk, alumna poet-teacher
reprinted from 2003–04 CPITS anthology

WHAT RAINS

— a half-sestina

When the French composer Satie died
they found two hundred umbrellas in his flat,
maybe to keep the clefs and notes from washing away
in the storms that rumbled under his roof.
In any case, his music turned out wet — the strings
welling up, falling over us like rain.

One long February it was snow that rained
into my life — a blizzard of innocence in the dead
of winter. Enough to loosen the taut strings
of my teenage daughters' hearts (their wonder flat
and dark, anger-drenched from toe to roof).
But that day we let the snow wash us away

down to the Niagara, whose icy white thunder washed away
the years. I watched them grow young again under a rain
of colored stars that shimmered above the rooftops —
a storm of fireworks reflected on snow. I could have died
right there, seeing them so alive, so silly, so flat-
out happy, dancing like puppets released from their strings.

Prartho Sereno, poet-teacher

SICK

I cannot go to school today,
Said little Peggy Ann McKay

I have a cold that is very uncommon.
It is much like the curse of Tutankhamen

My legs are bleeding, cold, and blue
If I go to school they might sue

My arms and legs are covered in lumps
I might have a severe case of the mumps

My phlegm is yellow and green
If I cough one more time you might see my spleen

My head hurts more than a hammer hitting a nail
If you look at my face it is very pale.

I don't think anything can help this sickness,
If you want you can ask a witness.

I have a fever and the flu
Cancer, and cystic fibrosis too.

My nails are cracked, my skin is too,
I think I may have swallowed some bad food.

My nose is stuffed too much to breathe
It's getting really hard to sneeze.

Oh! Today's a holiday
I guess I will go out and play!

Kian Sheik, sixth grade
Del Mar Hills Academy of Arts and Sciences, San Diego County
Kimberly Cunningham, classroom teacher
Christina Burress, poet–teacher

THE BEEKEEPER'S STORY

(for Anne Mudge, artist and naturalist)

Healing comes with the patient passage of time —
In their honey-house, her bees shuffle and spin
their sticky magic. She visits them each day.

Yet today, she worries, Why, when I opened the nest
did angry bees swarm and chase me down the hill?
Did I crush one when I dropped the lid?

Returning, she peers into the hive, finds five bees, diligent
as medics, clustered around an injured one. Some tug
and pull its legs until the crippled bee wobbles to its feet —
rises, and flies.

Seretta Martin, poet-teacher

TIDAL WAVES

we are the water moving between the walls
stirring flow into the depths below
leaving drops of ourselves in the ocean
some call human, a naked ministry
of particles and waves
reaching inward
like seeds of sun

we pool in classrooms, theaters, kitchens
we reach out and boil
hungry for the flesh
of our knowing
the place where families gather
without scattering, dissecting
ourselves with meaning
where we fathom more
than our words

we hold the feelings that won't evaporate
and we ride the tide of their awakening
washing ourselves raw
with the bliss of shadows undammed
of joy set free
where memory seeps into the groundswell
and fuses the covenant of these bodies

Yes, we will melt back into the stars
but first, let us moisten the ground with our tears.

Blake More, poet–teacher

HOW TO BE A DOG

Stick your tongue out.

Take quick, deep pants.

Don't stop when you're

excited.

Bark loudly when the

doorbell rings.

Wag your tail.

Kneel down on your hands.

Crawl as fast as you can.

Taste the dog food.

Don't use a toilet.

Chew up the couch.

Keltyn Viel, third grade
Hamilton Elementary School, Marin County
Lori Campbell, classroom teacher
Lea Aschkenas, poet-teacher

WHAT IS THIS PLACE?

Renaming Warner Springs

What is this place
with wibble-wobble walks
that lead you over the crest of a rise
or along a too-steep slant?
What is this map that shows oh so big grounds?
Pygmy buildings fool the scale.

This grove is almost quiet
but the Black-Headed Swoopers
are filling a tree across the gulch.
The trucks pass by on the road
with their rumble shifting gears.

This picnic table is under the grove of
Grey-Trunked Leaf Holders, sturdy in build
and tenacity. They shade a single Bolstered Pine,
which will always need a brace.

If the bank of the gully was comfortable,
I'd sit closer to the Optimistic Corn Rush.
I'd admire its silk-like frizz at the top
of its stalks. I'd try to name their color.

Cathy Barber, poet–teacher

MEMORIES OF LOYALTON

I remember the glassy creek and
swimming hole just behind my old house.
My friends and I would play at my Indian tipi
then go to the good old swimming hole.
We would play all sorts of games,
like mermaids, Indians, and fairies.
My reed tipi was right beside the creek.
We'd pretend to wash clothes and plates
in that comely water,
it was just about the happiest place to be.

The swimming hole was nice and deep
with crawdads all around.
When we brought our buckets
we'd catch them,
then just let them go back,
be free!

I remember the monkey tree
we used to climb by the deep cavern,
the great big field of lupines
that led to the path up the mountain.
We'd play castle and house up at those gloomy rocks.
When we came around
that place was full of happiness and cheer!

I remember it now, the day my dad said
we were to move to Oakhurst for my dad's new job.
I ran back to the creek and wept; ever so hard I wept.
But finally I was able to say goodbye
to that big, beautiful place.
I *will* always remember it, always.

Jocelyn Boe, fourth grade
After School Writing Club
Oakhurst Elementary School, Madera County
Mary Lee Gowland, poet-teacher

I DON'T BELONG

I'm not who you think I am;
I don't belong in the crowd or up in the front row,
I belong in the back away from life itself.

I don't belong with anyone here;
I don't belong with this crowd or this clique.

I'm a lone wolf,
Striking all who get in my way!

I walk alone through the halls
With no one by my side.

I don't belong.

Katie Chambers, seventh grade
Grizzly Hill School, Nevada County
Mr. Hickman, classroom teacher
Will Staple, poet–teacher

THE SALTY SEA

I am not a book of boredom
I want to discover joy, I have seen and lost it
I call it   I shout at it   I say come back
The salty smell of the sea of heartbreak fills the air
I hear the lonely people moan
The sorrow feeling comes to mind
The frustration builds and builds
Can you forget the name?
That name you loved and loved
You want the cookies of pleasure back
But they are long away from you
The taste of sweet sweet love fills your mind
Your heart's in two
One is with you
But the other is lost in the sea, that salty smelling sea
The Sea of Heartbreak
Dear Reader, forget the name!
And go into the sea of joy

Freddie Gordillo, sixth grade
Mission San Jose Elementary School, Alameda County
Norie Mainprice, classroom teacher
Mara Sheade, poet-teacher

A POEM OF HOPE

A poem isn't a rip in the sky
      where evil lives
A poem isn't a hint of darkness
      in a peaceful meadow
A poem is a faint light
      in a pitch black room
A poem is a familiar seed
      in a foreign land
A poem is a forgotten rose
      in a field of poison ivy
A poem is life
      in a graveyard

Brian Go, fifth grade
Mission San Jose Elementary School, Alameda County
Tina Warnert, classroom teacher
Mara Sheade, poet-teacher

THE OTHER SHOE

is always
the one
we fear will
drop.
Why not
worry about
the first shoe's
fall instead
so all we
have to dread
occurs
right off
the bat
and nothing
we decide
matters after
that.

Lois Klein, poet–teacher

VACATION

When I went to Vegas
people bang ding-donged
It sounded like a jungle.
In the hotel they slapped the walls
and buzzed like mosquitoes.
They rattled like snakes
all over the halls
In the pool, people crashed into each other
They looked retarded.
A man who looked like a gorilla
ripped a woman's shirt.
My mom quacked at me
I said, "You said what? What are you talking about?"
I screamed for help.
I thought people were hunting for me. Even my mom.

Lourdes Ballanes, eighth grade
Los Osos Middle School, San Luis Obispo County
Laura Schuberg, classroom teacher
Michael McLaughlin, poet-teacher

THERE HAS ALWAYS BEEN A SONG

for Talia

Kids swarm the street like a garden of bees
as the ice cream man makes music
down the block. Sun sweats
every forehead, every little lip.
I watch as you drip red
onto the grass, your chin.
Even your hair wears sticky juice.

Fifteen years and you drive away
with a CD blasting, suitcase full
of monologues and a friend's old guitar.
A punk-hair boy with an earring
and black nails will teach you how to strum.

You call from the dorm.
Three drunk roommates sing
in the background and offer you a bottle,
but you'd rather slurp a popsicle
than beer. Tonight you wrote a song.
That's why you called.
There has always been a song.

Shelley Savren, poet–teacher

MY WORLD

The music took me to the soft beach sand.
I rolled the ball left and right
and I smelled so hard I lifted myself into the tree.
That made my heart purple, and I sang to my heart.
Off the tree there grows a silver seaweed
that helps poor, lonely people.
The smell at the beach has a cinnamon smell
that bursts all day and all night.
The air feels prick, prick, prickly.
The prickles help you remember worries that you had.
The water has five mermaids in it that sing
so loud the sky turns bright yellow, so yellow it bursts.
The caterpillars sing and they play with drums.

Payton Alonzo, second grade
Brookside School, Marin County
Melissa Hartley, classroom teacher
Prartho Sereno, poet–teacher

I CAME FROM A LAND

I came from a land of singing and
dancing.

I am more positive I will be a piece
connected to a puzzle of success.

When I hear the beautiful songs of
Mexico my ears are jumping in
happiness.

The place where I came from there are
beautiful waterfalls and the trees are
wonderful.
The fruit tastes like a bit of sky.

Alejandra Sariana, fifth grade
Sheppard School, Sonoma County
Kirsten Valstad, classroom teacher
Claire Drucker, poet-teacher

MY HANDS

My hands turned into pineapple
Listening to dinosaurs
My breath turns into dinner
Voices dreaming through the forest
I look into the stars' eyes
Hawk and Coyote thought a long time about the spill
the glad dancing of my hands upon earth.

Ordee Martin, sixth–seventh grade
Melrose Leadership Academy, Alameda County
Ms. Davila, classroom teacher
Tobey Kaplan, poet–teacher

TASMANIAN WOLF

Come, come here, Tasmanian wolf.
You feel lovely velvet with leaves.
You smell like wild earth.
Your creator was the stars.
You're like the tiger with the most fire and the most obsidian.
You, you are soul waiting to be used.
You are the music waiting to get played.
You are the tadpole waiting to learn how to swim.
You are the pencil waiting to be sharpened.
You are my leader telling me where to go.
We are partners deciding where to go.

Sianna Moreno, third grade
Oak Grove School, Sonoma County
Peggy Heil, classroom teacher
Phyllis Meshulam, poet-teacher

STRATEGIES OF THE HEART

i punish you
with my indifference
that is not
indifference
it is
a child
of weeping anger
striking you
with silence
or neglect
and distance
   of reject
it is
a crack
in my person
breaking open
and
swallowing me
beyond

beyond
the gentleness
of love
to the wars
of doubt
   and insecurity

it is
a war
without
victor, or victory

Veronica Cunningham, poet–teacher
reprinted from *If Only for a Day*

THE FARMER'S BREAK

His rough hands pull weeds
for giant crops.

At break time
going inside, he finds

a loafing cow
instead of a soft couch.

Nathan Dawson, third grade
Canyon View Elementary, San Diego County
Sean Blake, classroom teacher
Seretta Martin, poet-teacher

SILENCIO

Silencio
Si–lencio
Si–Si–lencio
lencio–si

El silencio es un caracól
en mi garganta.
Silence is a snail in my throat
and a bullet in my mouth.

¡Callate! ¡Silencio!

Sitting on the porch
under the dark, cool evening
while everyone else sleeps
we speak of the world beyond.
Remembering our childhood
we tell stories about
the Day of the Dead,
el dia de los muertos,
and chant:
Somos la muerte!
Somos la muerte!

¡Callate! ¡Silencio!

Shoes fall like rain
when the others awake.
We say:
Everyone sleeps with the devil
and the night is an empty shell.
Full of *duendes y brujas.*
and pigs knocking at your door.
(group oinks)

¡Callate niño! ¡Silencio!

The dark night
a thousand crows covering the sky
and *coyotes locos*
are piercing the stars
with their howl
(group howls)

¡Callate! ¡Silencio!

The night stinks of sleep.
The dreams are like *vacas*
mooing at the moon.
(group moos)

¡Callate niño! ¡Silencio!

Don't you remember
what your grandfather told you.
Don't let a stray dog lick your hand
or you'll be lost forever in the night.
Those are not dogs
They are devils roaming
between life and death.
Run, child, run!
Don't let the barking dogs
come near.
(group barks)

¡Callate! ¡Silencio!

The night swallows
the faint whisper of wind.
People sing in their sleep.
The water drips.
Poets rest their bodies.
Tonight

no one watches.
The breath
in and out
in and out
and in my head

¡Callate niño!
Si . . .
Len . . .
Cio . . .
Shoooooo.

Luis Kong, alumnus poet–teacher
reprinted from 1993 CPITS anthology

Note: Audience participates by making the
animal sounds while the reader reprimands
them by yelling "¡Callate! ¡Silencio!"

MORNING PRAYER

This is the prayer
of torn paper
and burning limbs
of summer oak

This is the prayer
of smoke
and smoldering resin
that will never evaporate
completely from the sky

This is the prayer
for the absent swan
for the flightless wings
for the broken shells
for the mud-thick river

A prayer for the silent
a prayer for the shouting
a prayer for the disappeared
a prayer for the unborn

This is a prayer of simple
silence
from a heart on fire,
for every mother who
sends her children
out to meet this world
this morning.

Karen Lewis, poet-teacher

LAS GALLINAS RESERVOIR

As the Canada geese glide overhead
casting a shadow on the black-necked stilts,
my heart folds inward.
My heart becomes the shape of this pond.
My heart ripples with delight
as the shovelers swim in circles
scooping up algae for their meal.
My heart shouts for joy
as the white pelican resting on the bank
splays its enormous wings towards sunlight.
My heart recognizes the underbelly of the harrier
as if it were the palm of my own hand.
My heart is the rhythm of water
of air of winged creature.
My heart is the rhythm of tide
of moon of earth.
My body is the dance of elemental joy
here at the pond
where the geese glide over
the delicate black-necked stilts
wading in the water.

Terri Glass, poet–teacher

THE WOMEN ARE DANCING

Ahhhhh, what strange lights over my head
circling — grinding sand and gravel
into this precious mettle — the evening
starlight on their lips — flashing chimes
descending this zero-hour's gravity
splashing the storm's wind and rain —
Their sheer veils unfurl this clay landscape's
raw need of soil — mystifying sensuous spirit
shapes out of oak — elegant eyes: deer and wolves
dancing, they are dancing, dancing again —

The inner sense — henna and rose!
Perfume in this wind's crystal
owls richen their stars, fiery, passing —
in a clatter of limbs: winter blue oak
audible — scintillating laughter like
ouuuu-cougars purrrrrr-night's moist wisdom!
A flutter of wings — the planets align!
In indigo the moon's ripe horns, with silken veils
the women appear, liquid in the flame's glow
dancing, the women are dancing, dancing again —

Into our ink's brightest jewel:
the wound's deepest healing —
In this body's sacred circle:
at world axis, a crescent horizon
in the blade's balance, revolving
the crone's crown wisdom — Oh dancer
in my heart's purest, egg innocence — Ohhh
salubriously so saucy — campfire for a lover's arms
lavender-gold flame — dancing, she is dancing
dancing the dream, the women are dancing —

Chris Olander, poet–teacher

STANDING IN FRONT OF CROWDS

Shyness follows me everywhere I go
the hooded jacket, dark as coal,
covers her face.
She doesn't talk in class
just sits, avoiding eye contact.
"Get some friends, participate more," I tell her.
Shyness doesn't reply. Remains silent.
Her mouth, a closed zipper.
She never speaks to anyone.
Nothing comes from her mouth
no murmur, no sigh.
She walks far behind groups of students
always runs away when people get close.
She hides behind buildings avoiding everyone.
Shyness always stands in the back
or in dark places, where no one can see her, motionless.
Her hands are pale like an ill person's skin
because no sunlight can reach them.
Shyness follows me everywhere I go.

Leyna Arroyo, seventh grade
Farb Middle School, San Diego County
Alison Nayoski, classroom teacher
Johnnierenee Nelson, poet-teacher

SUISUN

Every August
Down by the Suisun wharf
Into the flat empty fields
The carnival tumbled

Out of the powdery dirt
Bloomed the big tent, the sideshows
The games of shooting and tossing
The dissonant symphony of calliope, laughter, and screams

Out of the bright dust
Rose the miracle of the Ferris wheel
Pastel baskets of arms and legs
Circling up to the stars

And down again, down
down to the broken families

Down to the broken families
And down again, down

Circling up to the stars
Pastel baskets of arms and legs
Rose the miracle of the Ferris wheel
Out of the bright dust

The dissonant symphony of calliope, laughter, and screams
The games of shooting and tossing
Bloomed the big tent, the sideshows
Out of the powdery dirt

The carnival tumbled
Into the flat empty fields
Down by the Suisun wharf
Every August

Judy Bebelaar, poet–teacher

LULLABY

i know what R says is true:

the infant takes on all
the unconscious conflict
that resides within the mother's psyche

[

                                                                    ]

then, the conversation lightens, a little:

your daughter is human with human problems

        i brush my girl's hair, the ritual symbolizing
        respect for her ideas
        as i do, she screams:

        you're not careful!
        you're not careful!

Dana Teen Lomax, poet–teacher

THE TASTE OF WHIPPED MIST

Silver swoops above the snowy plain.
She wears a strapless dress made of glowing lights
and carries a handbag made of the finest spider silk.
She was born on the puffiest cloud.
Her mother is the finest seamstress
and her father a brave knight.
For breakfast she eats bark waffles and whipped mist.
When she is sad, she lies on her cloud bed
and silently weeps tears of diamond rain.
She dreams of living in the light of love.

Meg Organ, third grade
Oak Manor School, Marin County
Erika Smith, classroom teacher
Prartho Sereno, poet-teacher

PATTERNS OF THE PAST

(for Finland)

Bread
and the small white fish of the lake

Do you go with me
to the red pine-wood church?
Thin white wafers
at the altar,
dark drink to cleanse the soul.

Wind in the white nights
unnerves the silent glow.
Warm the bones
white under the flesh,
at sauna's hot stones,
at the kitchen's heated stove.

The family gathers in the large room.
Silence shows respect.
Stories and singing lighten the time.
Berry bread,
nut bread,
sugar in the coffee,
cheese baked black on the oven's
lowest shelf.

Learn to be
quiet as a winter mouse,
learn to fly
Outdoors in the long summer sun.

Store green under your skin,
Weave fire into the rug.
Red cushions in white snow,
Bells under black branches.

Grace Marie Grafton, poet-teacher

DREAM AND COLOR

Many colors surround me

Day and night
Haunting and enchanting me
A musty gray hovers above me on a powerful winter day
The marvelous blue of the spring sky twinkles for the world
It bounces on a ray of sun.

Blue jays peck into the heart of small dusty acorns
Ripe enough to show a hint of brown
That every acorn will someday overflow with.

Ruby red slippers sparkle and glow as Dorothy
Skips happily down the sacred yellow brick road
Protected by the power of good
Yellows bounce through the sky
Tickling the cheeks of those who are cold
A queen waves a delicate hand to her citizens
A sapphire glimmers in the sunlight
Illuminating its spot on her crown.

A falling leaf of orange and brown
Drifts to the rich soil, its birthplace
A blue roan gallops alongside a trickling brook
Slowly being swallowed by the streaming colors of the land
Slowly disappearing as colors collide and mix
Returning to a background of dream and color

Salem Davern, fourth grade
Tamalpais Valley Elementary School, Marin County
Kate Kellman, classroom teacher
Michele Rivers, poet-teacher

FOR ALEXANDRA GIANNA

There is that time when kids
Outage their parents
It happens at different times
Depending on just how young
The parents purport to be
Or how wise the kids are
It doesn't take Saint Cecilia to know this

My youngest son
Has become the image
Of my late beloved father
The way my son holds
His newborn daughter
Leads me back to my birth

The look in my son's eyes is
The look in my father's eyes
And probably my grandfather's eyes
Life continues in circles
Circles more perfect than bubbles blown
Into the winter sun

Yvonne Mason, poet-teacher

THE BELLY OF THE VOLCANO EXPLODES

the tennis ball's glowing ears listen to silence.
the fiery belly of the volcano explodes. the tongue
shoots into a goal immediately. the mouth drinking
poison and not dying. the legs doing something hard, but they
manage. a windy belly playing star wars on
PlayStation 3. a shiny moon watching Indiana Jones.
an electric shadow saying yo yo yo yipi i yo.
a weird elf sings hip hop. an animal crashing
everywhere in a person's body, but can't get out.

Ido David Baruch, fourth grade
Miraloma Elementary School, San Francisco County
Kay Kirman, classroom teacher
Sally Doyle, poet-teacher

FOUR SHORT POEMS

             hi I say
               waving to my friends but
      we have to say goodbye
for I inform you, I am moving
of course you'll keep on walking
      on the glorious road of happiness
           for this city is
               busy of glory and wonders.

A parade of ferocious fireworks
flash and flicker in the enormous
sky and hold the love as breakable
as ceramic given by the heart.

   A talented silver cat wears
its socks and dress we call fur.
It sinks its feet in the shiny
snow and has a blast.

Sandy tosses a nickel in the
crooked jukebox of the strange
place and exits. She has to go
with her unstoppable curiosity
so her blessing always exits.

Maggie Phillips, fourth grade
After School Program
Highlands Elementary School, San Mateo County
Cathy Barber, poet–teacher

THE TEACHER OBSERVES TREES WITH THE FIRST GRADE

Look, over there —
Is it a dogwood or a maple,
the teacher asks,
under the impression
she's leading this discussion.

The branches look like legs of a horse
running into thunder —
A girl in front answers,
forgetting to raise her hand.

The teacher points to another,
showing off its deciduousness.
Someone explains:
It has a nice coat of wind and rain.

The teacher taps the windowpane
and asks whoever's listening
to please locate their favorite.

All eyes turn to the hummingbird,
hovering at the fence —
Never mind the tree in full bloom.

Karen Benke, poet-teacher

SECRET OF THE CHILDREN

Swish, swish.
>Turn left.
Swish, swish.
>Turn right.
Swish, swish.
>Up and out of bed.
Swish, swish.
>The child's room is empty.
Swish, swish.
>Yet filled with the rustling
>>of curtains.
Swish, swish.
>She's gone.
Swish, swish.
>Up to the stars.
Swish, swish.
>Follow.
Swish, swish.
>Watch them dancing,
>>dancing.
Swish, swish.
>Come, come home.
Swish, swish, swish.

Megan Twain, third grade
Lafayette Elementary School, San Francisco County
Dianna Mays, classroom teacher
Susan Herron Sibbet, poet-teacher

THIS LAND

> — *new words to Woody Guthrie's song,*
>   *written after the Presidential election*

This land is your land; this land is my land;
We all can vote here; we all are free here.
We all can smile here; lucky we live here!
        This land is made for you and me.

We come together; we've made it better.
We help each other, sisters and brothers.
We all can learn more than we knew before:
        This land is made for you and me.

We all can sing here; we all can dance here;
We all can play here; we all have friends here.
This place is your home; this place is my home:
        This land is made for you and me.

We sing together and play together.
We all have talents, so there's a balance.
We are so happy; we're one big family:
        This land is made for you and me.

We can have peace here; we can find love here.
This is our country; here we can live free.
We all can join hands to work for our lands:
        This land is made for you and me.

We have enough to eat; we've got shoes for our feet.
We can feel safe here; it's what we make it here.
We make decisions; we make revisions:
        This land is made for you and me.

We work for fairness; we work for kindness.
We all are readers; we choose our leaders.
We all can speak out; we all can shout it out:
        This land is made for you and me!

        This land is made for you and me!

fourth grade students
Los Olivos School School, Santa Barbara County
Bridget Baublits, classroom teacher
Teresa McNeil MacLean, poet–teacher

AMERICAN SUMMATIONS

Think back for a moment. Chicano boys do not write about the world. Is this true? Chicana girls are not supposed to write about the world — everyone should know this. Right? I am serious.

The word *Razorshell* is not part of the Chicano or Chicana vocabulary. Neither is *piano*. I mean the *real* piano. The *world as piano*. How about sound? Hear it. Is it the cry of a crackling mast: the spirit or moan inside the left region of the chest? The reporter of the *Chronicle* never mentioned it to you. And if he did, he said three words like *desolation* and *despair* and another "D" word like *deportation*. He said news like HOW THE MEXICAN GARDENER WILL HAVE TO GO BACK HOME BECAUSE HE NEEDS THE RIGHT PAPERS, visa, etc. Think on it.

Mex-boys and Mex-girls are always getting caught w/out papers. And back they go, again: the myth of Sisyphus-Tijuana. The American summation of our reality. No papers. Much less no pencil. Write? Write what? Maybe a note to someone back home, an aunt in Atzcapozalco or a feeble grandfather in Michoacan where they make the best guitars, the best sombreros and where they grow the best marijuana. Better yet, we write messages of distress (antother "D" word): earthquakes and border massacres, or a fanciful paragraph or two about mother's embroidery. I am not kidding. Never the world. Mundo=Never. Think never.

Have you ever seen a Chicana girl busy writing about the world? Have you read her world words?

Partial Synopsis:

Three acres, burnt, scorched electric, children — the autumn of objections. I release. Crucifix colossus sweating. Bulbous convent. Very good. Nice. Years and years I loved you.

But this — as you can see — smells of that old spray of summations we were talking about: petulant inner-directed narratives of martyrdom.

The *Chronicle* reporter.
The Courtroom recorder.
The University admissions restorer.

They want you to believe these wary condensations. No need to be more politically precise about it. Because, you see, the fact of the matter is that Chicano boys and girls need not bother writing about the world.

Think again.

Razorshell is a beautiful word: a crystal ball with hazel eyes inside gazing out. Looking at you. The eyelashes cut through the glass walls. As the eyes blink an incredible tear of joy pours an aquamarine landscape. A star-lit system crashes. A serpent snaps its golden snout revealing twin opal fangs in the night inside a little house, a very little house full of busy brown hands clapping in unison as the planet sleeps. Have you read about this? I doubt it.

We write.

We write parallelogram, trapezoid and rhomboid shards, puzzles, pyramids with red stairways to the ocean. The womb. The loom. The wave. The new moon growing out of our fingernails glowing. Can you hear it?

Juan Felipe Herrera, alumnus poet-teacher
reprinted from 1988 CPITS anthology

I, TOO, CAN RIDE A HORSE

(after Langston Hughes)

I, too, can ride a horse.
I am the best in the class.
They think I am unsafe and not ready.
But I can canter,
And trot,
And walk easily.
Tomorrow,
I'll race ahead of everyone.
Nobody'll dare
Say to me,
"Follow directions!"
Then.
Besides,
They'll see I am a fiery speed demon
And be ashamed.
I, too, can ride free!

Anika Horn, third grade
Brookside School, Marin County
Laurel Ferrari, classroom teacher
Dana Teen Lomax, poet-teacher

PENSADORA

> — *Luanda Angola*

Students posed questions
    we could not answer for them.
    What to do about so many poor?
        Neighborhood canyons of trash?
        And if your friend, whose family
            was lost in the war, is losing his faith,
            what do you tell him to keep
                him going? If your girlfriend is pregnant
                    and she wants to lose the baby,
            what should you do? Heaven? Love
        at first sight? Ghosts? Conversations roved
        and circled. When someone says "nothing
    to lose" she still really means everything
    she just no longer values a thing.
    The kids changed the questions
    but it's the same one
I've been asking myself
for years. How now?
    Where to go from here?
    In the classroom I see
        an army of *pensadoras,*
        hunkered down with their thoughts.
            Pensadoras common as guns,
            visible everywhere. Thinkers line
                town shop shelves, silhouette fabric
                    and dishes, face out from city walls,
                hold their heads in homes. *Pensadora's*
        back curves like a wing, balancing,
        bent with history, knees tucked
    to chest, elbows on knees,
    hands on head, heart cradled, forever
    gazing forward. *Pensadoras* —
    guardians of ashes
and a phoenix on the rise.

Marissa Bell Toffoli, poet-teacher

RIGHT BACK HOME

We were out in the dark
at dusk with the wind
when the moon snapped in half
and fell on our car
when half rolled away
with the wind howling loud
with a crash and a thud
and a smooth but big splash.
The other half went down.
I saw all the fish
and a shark with a fin.
We went down so deep
there wasn't a sound.
We swam up real fast
and took a breath for our lives
and walked back home
slow and quiet.

Jonathan Sessa, fourth grade
Pierpont Elementary, Ventura County
Angela Werth, classroom teacher
Shelley Savren, poet-teacher

MR. BELLA DANCES THE FLAMENCO

Mr. Bella in his third-grade classroom
of Christmas lights, guitar
leaning against the blackboard,
pulls dark chestnut castanets,
polished by fingers and palms,
from his desk —
"These are old and small,"
he says, "and I have not practiced."

But in that first beat
is a tongue tapping
a thousand songs.
Our shoulders quiver.
His feet–ball–heel–ball–heel
ball–heal–flat.
Pencils rattle.
Our heads erect like the young
learning:
    this is how you catch the worm
                listen for snakes
                smell for seals
Arms now —
    "Hands heavy, rise last.
    This is how you open —
    A flower closing
    pressing the walls."

Mr. Bella turns his hips
    TLACK TLACK TLACK
Head and neck
    Fingers articulating architecture
        of India — TLACK TLACK TLACK

"Chest high, proud"
That is Spanish — tall as
the wall clock Ticka Tock a Ticka —
Ticka Tock Tock

12 beats — go —

We jump from our skins

He's out the room through
    the windows
    hips smooth as honey

Take us with!
Do we have to eat the bread,
the oranges, drink the water
    before we dance?

No. Rise! It's in your mind
Go, feel it — cry of a bird
with a wound in its throat —
the smallest of raindrops
from the darkest cloud

Catch it, says Mr. Bella.

Fly — fly out the windows
    with me.

Susan Terence, poet-teacher

WOMAN

I dreamt one day to embrace this essence of woman.
My whole life all I've known is her.
Woman raised, fed, provided,
Taught me the things no one else could,
Managed to make me strong even at her weakest,
And wrapped me in her arms
When no one else would.

When stuck in the depths of war
She fought with me,
And lifted me to victory.
A life saved, a life defined by woman.
She said, "Never to get too down because
Tomorrow you still have to get up."
I held her hand as she battled the incurable,
Looked into her fearless eyes
And knew that no matter how far apart we are,
We will grow. And that this thing called change
Is eagerly awaiting our arrival.

Nothing and no one inspires me the way she does.
I see her on the front page of campaign news,
Or sitting in her "best view of the city" office,
Marching her way down the streets with
Something to say, working the nine to five,
Then overtime, holding life in her very arms,
Promising her whole self to them.
I see her beating every odd set out in front of her.

Her words cling to my heart as she
Fills me with wisdom beyond anything I've ever known.
A stunning light that shines on me from this
Ancient sky they said was the limit,

But she is the sky and all the stars put together
Can't amount to her greatness.
Because she and her,
You and I, us and we, are
Magnificently, beautifully,
Woman.

Roshawnda Bettencourt, twelfth grade
Oakmont High School, Placer County
Judy Geduldig, classroom teacher
Chris Olander, poet-teacher

EPIPHANY, FOR JL

Let's just see what comes
on this semi-sunny Wednesday
in the school, in the visiting nurse's room
where I, the poet, attend the young
poets —
This one is slender, a boy with hair in his eyes
his eyes a small gate which still opens
out, but my eyes see his
thinking about locking the outside
out
Has he been barged in on?
Have his eyes seen what they wished
they hadn't?
Will he, behind them, ever tell
all the ways he's dreamed of locking
himself free
from the sorrow he's witnessed
from the anger he's seen ride
people as if they were unbroken
broncos
Who is this boy in front of me
chin in right hand
left hand stabbing paper
as his eyes have stabbed me
cautiously
as I ask him to let me see
why blindness sometimes invites
why he knows darkness
and its cool safety
vanishing

Eva Poole-Gilson, poet-teacher

BLUE MIDNIGHT MELODIES

1

my mother in an almost-trance
her strong fingers
in red brown clay
weeding plantain   stubborn wild grasses
she could make anything grow
savory wax beans
sour to the core rhubarb
lush sweet corn
half a dozen varieties of crinkly lettuce
stuffed our endless summer
sandwiches

she was happiest in the garden
her palette riotous
   ochre
      russets
         sizzling cinnabar
            emerald and lime
her olive skin baked brown
while I lay reading
cellophane-covered books
from the bookmobile

2

nighttime the garden came alive
a-hum
with electric-breathing-upward-moving songs
symphony
of crickets and
cicadas
zshh *zshh*
  zshh
liquid curtains of amber fire flies
blinking their coded SOS

silky toads
lime-green Ichabod Crane
praying mantis lurching
in slow motion
one thin leg at a time

in heavy humidity
I'd sit
silently
at one with corn and earth

who knows
what ancient shamans may have
leaned into secret cornstalk shadows
on those honeyed summer moon nights
whispering blue
    midnight melodies
        remembering me
then gliding away
on luminous rays of birch bark

Beth Beurkens, poet-teacher

WORDS GONE OVERBOARD

My student disapproves of
Allen Ginsberg's radical
ramblings   scribbles
out a whole paragraph
of his essay on writing —
John, we all go too far
wandering aimlessly
our curiosity pulls us
into alligator pits and
heaven — the most outrageous
today guides us home
tomorrow   but
I don't tell him then
but wait till the end of the semester
when he will write his wild
outrageous masterpiece —
till he stumbles in the
jungle . and rises slowly
from the dark —

Claire Blotter, poet-teacher

VALENTINE'S DAY IN THE EIGHTH GRADE

Outside, the rhythmic thump of basketballs on asphalt
and yelling and screaming from gym class.
Inside, the kids lean over their ragged scraps of paper,
writing a word, crossing it out, writing it over again.

Lining up, the rows of eighth-grade boys push each other into lockers
to express the love that dare not say its name.
The girls are writing volumes. They favor light green ink, or purple.
The popular ones have gifts of teddy bears on the corners of their desks,

or a single rose, wrapped with a twist of babies' breath,
sheathed chastely in plastic.
The air is red with the beauty of their lips pursed in thought,
or hung half-open in the slackness of desire.

Pain hums a half-note below Romance
who is stalking the room with her bow and arrows, looking for easy prey.
She finds it, sure, but not so many as Heartbreak
who has already drawn a net around the quieter ones.

I measure my own strength
against the weight of the questions I carry
and find the questions heavier than ever this year,
although my heart is wider.

Oh, Love, my arms are tired.
I would like to set you down, on a scarred desk,
gently, in front of one of the younger ones.
They still know everything.

Instead, I walk up and down between rows
chanting my grocery list of poetry ideas.
"Where does Loneliness live? What does Truth wear?
Who does Love like to hang around with?"

And Tony J, who up till now has shown a genius
only for making farting noises with his hand and asking questions like
"Mr. Messier, how do you spell 'puke'?" says "Love?
That's easy. Love will hang out with anyone."

Alison Luterman, alumna poet-teacher
reprinted from 1998 CPITS anthology

HOW TO MAKE A MOCKINGBIRD BE QUIET

To make a mockingbird be quiet
you must put it in a cold cage, *brr, brr,*
brr. But that does not help. You
must kill it then. Hear the *whir, whir, whir*
of the ax. But then hear the soft,
scared, beautiful delicate song of a
mockingbird. It is a sin to kill a
mockingbird.

Tea Bianchi–Bellfor, fifth grade
Alvarado Elementary School, San Francisco County
Anastasia Pickens, classroom teacher
Florencia Milito, poet-teacher

BRAG

My eyes are the drills you see in old-fashioned cartoons
they burrow, uncurl, burn
they see what few other eyes see —
     vague dreams of Bushmen in Tanzania, of Inuit, of Antarctica,
     & the amniotic fluid of a flying fish's wings
they see things, they see things
My eyes change ribbons in women's hair to white doves,
turn dirt into diamonds, crab legs into fiddle bows,
they see things no other eyes have seen
bright raven wings on Andes peaks & honey glinting in a bee's beak

These eyes can call a rainstorm by a small glance to the sky
These eyes can make the earth turn 2,000 revolutions in a day —
     sunrises & sunsets blast each time a child blinks

And when I shake my finger, the seven seas will rattle
And when I flex my wrist, the mountain grass will tremble
     when I nod my head, each iris from Timbuktu to Peru nods with me
And North & South switch places on the poles
And the Milky Way disperses
And when I step out my door, each dead poet rises to greet me
     stars get up & dance, stars put on their running shoes & do relays

And when I open my mouth, sea anemones crawl to land to be my
     megaphones
     All ears tune to the exact rise & fall of my libretto
and when I open my mouth, wolves will howl in accolades

And when I speak
     every movement will stop
     the earth will stand still, even the dirt will hear

     You will not hear a pin drop

And when I speak
     Senators will listen
     Presidents will listen
     Mothers & Fathers & Children will listen

And when I speak
     the world will change

Eleni Sikelianos, alumna poet-teacher
reprinted from 1993 CPITS anthology

WORDS

my hands turn into wind
listening to the river
my breath turns into water
voices dreaming through mountains
I dream of you flying
I look into the mountain
Hawk and Coyote thought a long time about the songs
   of the forest people
Houses made of paper
Everything talks about poetry.
I was trying to lock the door of darkness
I heard the voice of the sky
the first music of the anger
I made houses of paper
Everything talks with poetry
I climb to the moonlight with the gold rope
I saw the angels smiling below

Wafa Abdullah, sixth–seventh grade
Melrose Leadership Academy, Alameda County
Ms. Davila, classroom teacher
Tobey Kaplan, poet–teacher

EARTH

I feel stepped on
I see the moon
I hear ocean waves
I wonder why I'm so warm
I touch the cold lonely space
I pretend I am as big as the sun
I worry that I will burn up
I want to be healthy
I dream I am a human
I hope I will survive
I try to get myself noticed
I say I'm healthy
I am Earth

Alexandra Strehlow, third grade
Ormondale Elementary School, San Mateo County
Daphna Woolfess, classroom teacher
Karen Llagas, poet-teacher

EMBRACING WATER

for Lake Ediza

Between darkness mountains
and a brash white outpouring over rocks
(banks sticky with purple & green)
a lake, queen among mountain lakes,
captures snow melt in her bowl;
a lake impossible to hold

though she can grasp the moon with one hand,
with the other, fish for the sun.
She calls me at dawn; on her quivering
blue-black belly, swirls her encryptions.
The golden fish jumps into view.
Mountains brighten to maroon

medieval minarets, a fan,
like a wooden xylophone struck by light,
slowly rubbed warm with polish.
Humbler formations glowingly buttress sky.
A bird instructs, *look at me,*
look at every every leaf.

Long-awaited lake, scrambling sky & rock,
olive-ochre-tan under glass,
sucklings at your shores,
silver, wind-scratched,
I ask only a small keepsake in words
a drop of evidence like liquid quartz.

Phyllis Meshulam, poet-teacher

PURE HAPPINESS

I was happy every minute
    and am, even now,
        every minute happy

and should an unavoidable cloud
    appear upon the vast horizon
        happy I to endure it

and tears, happy
        in this exquisite release

and should there be an ache
    between my breasts
    bless me holy mother
        for I have a heart!

Will Staple, poet–teacher

SUSAN'S MUSES

Alarmina   The muse of waking early

Caffeina   The muse of making strong coffee

Persistina   The muse of sitting in the chair

Patienza   The muse of empty waiting

Silencia   The muse of quiet hope

Pushapena   The muse of putting the pen to paper

Focusina   The blind and deaf muse of writing no matter what

Finishina   The muse of knowing when to end

Susan Herron Sibbet, poet–teacher

THE SHADOW CHAPTER

On the blackboard the teacher writes:
Techniques for the Week —
Read the Shadow Chapter. Just then
a shadow from a passing cloud
enters the classroom
to teach the sixth grade
about form and substance
and how it can all
disappear. There is
a noticeable hush in the room,
a deepening hue.
The shadow reveals
that it cannot give them the answers
to the quiz they are about to take,
but the quiz doesn't require answers
only questions. There is an invisible word
you can't see yet. Pay attention.
There's a Chinese dragon who knows your name.
The teacher sees that the students are distracted.
She snaps the ruler against the desk
and begins counting down from ten.
The students are focused, but it's as if
they are studying a voice behind the wall,
another language, or perhaps music.
They are not following the time line
thumbtacked around the room.
1.3 billion years ago the universe begins.
The students are listening somewhere else.
Their minds aren't made up yet.
The white board is shiny and glacial.
New elements float through the room
not on the periodic table. The students, already brilliant,
are moving past Paleolithic and millenniums.
The shadow blesses them and is gone.

Kathy Evans, poet-teacher

AUTUMN

Her hair falls,
a swirl of marigold.
A hushed wind blows.
Leaves drift around her.
She smiles a sweet rosy smile,
beautiful pink against her pale skin.
Her light green eyes flash with excitement
as she twirls in the fallen leaves.
She stops and gazes at the
stormy gray sky,
a beautiful picture forever
embedded in my mind.
Autumn, my little sister.
Forever,
Autumn.

Winter Paris, eighth grade
John Muir School, San Diego County
Chet Hancock, classroom teacher
Jackleen Holton, poet-teacher

ODE

You want them to write
an ode, a love song
to whatever delights
or defines them, and all they want
is to mock the drone
of the math teacher stuck in the fifties,
whose pants are too short and socks
are white. Or they want
to rattle off the slang
for their greatest curse,
their favorite sport,
the body parts that possess them
and which they yearn to possess,
the latest secret code of sex
they figure you can't decipher.
Or they want, simply,
to be left alone. Look
at this one, huddled inside
his arctic hood, asleep and slumped
toward the open window, explorer
of the other way. Or this one,
who recoils from being made
to speak the little she loves
for fear it will vanish, as so much
already has by her sixteenth year.
You too are afraid: that you don't have
what it takes to touch them
the way they need to be touched,
which is why you want them to do for themselves, praise
whatever sustains them, whatever
is good and doesn't go away.
And so, how can you not love them
when they answer with anti-odes:
to homework and take-homes,

to slow death by boredom, to the unspeakable
acts their bodies have endured for years
and for which they are only beginning
to find the pathetic and necessary words?
And on your last day, how can you
not love it when the quietest one
is changing at his locker
in a crowded hallway, teasing
the girls as he drops his pants,
the girls pretending they're in shock,
how can you hear him sing,
almost to himself, I'm the one
you love to hate — young boy smile
on a young man face, the old joy
of self-love still intact — how can you
hear him sing and not want to sing along,
not want to smile back?

Thomas Centolella, alumnus poet-teacher
reprinted from 1996 CPITS anthology

CORRUPTED SOUL

I am a man that learned to trust no one
I am a man who begins to comprehend
I am a man looking around, ain't no one around,
I am alone
I am a man listening on how I be tripping
How these guys coming around
      A bunch of them claiming to be your boys
      Your dogs breaking the laws
I am a man calling them pretenders, fakers
I am a man shaking the hand of a man
That is ready to take ya break ya
Only pretending to be a g
I am a man that is knowing
I am a man that's showing no props and no one to trust
I am a man who thinks hanging alone is a must
I am a man that believes I'll get em' and
      Wet em', forget em' and let em' affect me
      Makin' em' respect me.
I am a man.

Larry, eleventh grade
Providence High School, Ventura County
Lucia Lemieux, poet-teacher

APPETIZERS AT HURRICANE KATE'S

With this brushstroke I me wed.
I paint the past a cherry red.
Red for life, red for death,
cherry syrup on my breath.

For my father in his grave,
my heavymetal brother Dave,
my nephews surging into life,
my Grail quest: the perfect wife.

Red flows through my sunburnt heart:
broken poems, liquid art.
I'd like to say it's all been gold;
perhaps I may when I am old.

Splash some ketchup on this meal —
make me taste it, make me feel.
Cut another splendid scar.
With your death I me war.

Life keeps oozing from its pores.
We keep asking for more s'mores.
Go ahead, bite something sweet,
angel caked with mad, red meat.

Daniel Zev Levinson, poet-teacher

1986

My father crashed his car
after nights in the hospital
without sleep, anesthetizing
spines. I turned eight
and afternoon cartoons

were interrupted by the president
to talk for hours on the curfew
and the communists. My sister
and I learned not to insist
on endings. My father stopped

smoking. What I missed most:
the shine of rice paddies
in the late afternoons, us stopped
on the side of the road, my father
in scrubs, smoking; my father,

who long ago rolled down
his car window to scream *puta!*
to a rally for a dictator, my father
painting flat landscapes now —
the Golden Gate bridge lying

beside the ocean, fruit pasted
on the table — squinting across from me,
still learning how to fake distance.

Karen Llagas, poet–teacher

HOUSEBOAT HAIKUS

He rides his bike down
the dock, his shadow pedals
across the bay.

Highlighted by the moon,
two iridescent pigeons
kiss atop my roof.

The egrets are white
giraffes, stalking prey across
this wet savanna.

At low tide, the earth,
a treasure chest. Sunken ships
and oily rainbows.

After the downpour,
sun slants against the dock, steam
rises like a dream.

Lea Aschkenas, poet-teacher

A NEIGHBORHOOD BOY

i live quite near to a boy
who kills people

he is fourteen years old

young enough for me
to remember when
he in the fifth grade
was a most wonderful poet

you could see his brilliance
shining with the dark energy
of a universe expanding

he neatly filled both sides
of the lined newsprint sheet
as he took the color black and
dressed it in all the possibilities
his ten-year-old mind could imagine

it was magic and sleek
it was thunder and song
alive, powerful
and yes it was
beautiful

he wrote his poem
and then asked
to read his words out loud —
voice strong and clear
purposeful and steady

he shone brightly then
brighter than so many
of his classmates

some of whom
he may now shoot at

some of whom
may now shoot at him

youth together taking
the majesty of the night
and turning it into
sirens of misery and blood

i live quite near to a boy
who was born a poet
and now turns black
into the sound
of semi-automatic rounds
clattering across the mall
a pop, a whistle
a death wheeze
a mother's sobs
a tear dropped into oil

who was it then
who taught him black
as nothing but
caged and uncaged
field holler, whip groan
bar clang, lock nod
shake em up
shake em down
crack that back
bend and spread

who took his smooth obsidian
and ground it into gunpowder

devorah major, poet-teacher

CONSIDER COMPASSION

Consider the story of life.
How it began, who it touched.
Consider the war in the grass
Beetle and spider
Snake and mouse
Consider the child who suffers
The man who labors hatless in the sun
The woman who begs in the road
Consider the twig, song, rain, trees
Consider bread
Consider compassion
The choices we wake to each morning
and lie down with at night

Gail Newman, poet-teacher

COMPASSION

Waiting for the light to change,
I stand on the southwest corner
of Bush and Montgomery Streets.
The gray chill of an August morning in San Francisco.

I look down at the dachshund puppy,
tied to a lamppost, sitting atop newspaper
piled on a red plastic crate.
He is shivering in the chill and I think
"poor thing." I think about taking
some of the newspaper from beneath him
to make a cover for him. I think
of holding him, using my body heat
to warm him. I think how sad it is
he must sit out there day after day.

I don't see the two men
standing a few feet away, chatting.
Their dirty denim pants, jackets
out of place in the sea of suits.
I do not think "poor thing"
about the man who has been sleeping
in some doorway all night.
A blanket and this dog the only shields
between him and the world. I do not think
of bringing him blankets, clothes, food.
I do not think of touching him, or even
acknowledging his existence,
as I think of bending
to pet his dog.

Mara Sheade, poet-teacher

POLISH

I hear my
great-grandmother speak
Polish to me in
the night.

In the distance I hear
whales splashing
in the water

for the language
I am
hearing that is deep down in my heart
and I do not know.
I am learning
it.

I hear the fish
in the ocean.

The Alaskan language
at the bottom
is waiting to
rise.

Auggie Buschman, fourth grade
Helen Lehman Elementary School, Sonoma County
Cynthia Sumrall, classroom teacher
Pamela Raphael Yezbick, poet-teacher

A MAGICAL WINTER

I have the power to have a magical winter.
The river is shallow, but Christmas is not.
When time stops, everything stops but Christmas.
The crimson bird likes to play at a wintery mountain.
I dream that snow will fall down on the earth.
The winter eagle will keep on discovering
what winter really means.

Angus Li, fourth grade
Richmond District After School Collaborative
George Peabody Elementary School, San Francisco County
Claudia Dudley, poet-teacher

BLACK'S DREAM

Black slowly drifts into a large forest
full of oak trees being pushed by the wind.
He wears a shirt made of shadows.
His pants were made out of fern leaves;
his socks were made out of dragon scales
that weighed less than a feather.
All of his clothes felt as soft as lion's fur.
He was born in a tall oak tree;
he ate the bark and roots of the tree.
His dad was an oak tree
and his mom was a woodland spirit.
He eats roots, flowers, and leaves
and he drinks from a spring of cold blue water.
He also drinks the nectar of flowers.
When he is sad he goes up
into his tree house in a tall tree.
His friends are the magical animals of the forest,
like unicorns and dragons.
He dreams of becoming a spirit like his mother.
He loves his life.

Owen Waite, third grade
Oak Manor School, Marin County
Erika Smith, classroom teacher
Prartho Sereno, poet–teacher

POET-TEACHER CONTRIBUTOR BIOS

Opal Palmer Adisa | CPITS alumna poet-teacher | Opal Palmer Adisa was nurtured on cane-sap and the oceanic breeze of Jamaica. An award-winning poet and prose writer, Dr. Adisa has twelve titles to her credit, including the novel *It Begins With Tears* (1997), proclaimed by Rick Ayers as one of the most motivational works for young adults. Adisa taught with CPITS from 1982–88, but has been a guest poet in the schools throughout the years, and as recently as 2007. Her most recent title is *I NAME ME NAME* (2007).

Molly Albracht Sierra | Sonoma County | Molly Albracht Sierra received her MFA from San Francisco State University, where she has also taught creative writing. Her work has appeared in *Volt, New American Writing, The Oxford Review,* and other literary journals. She was the recipient of the 580 Split 2006 Poetry Prize and received the Browning Society Poetry Award in 2002.

Lea Aschkenas | Marin County | Lea Aschkenas has been teaching with CPITS since 2001. She is the author of *Es Cuba: Life and Love on an Illegal Island* (Seal Press, 2006). Other writings can be found in the books *The Best Women's Travel Writing 2006, Havana Noir, Travelers' Tales Cuba, Travelers' Tales Central America, The Unsavvy Traveler,* and *Two in the Wild.* In June 2009, she served as the writer-in-residence at Can Serrat Arts Centre outside Barcelona. Visit her at www.leaaschkenas.com.

Cathy Barber | San Mateo County | Cathy Barber is president of the Board of CPITS and a poet-teacher. She has an MA from CSU Hayward. Her poetry and prose have appeared in dozens of publications, including *Pearl, AIM, Ballyhoo Stories,* and *Tattoo Highway.* Her work has been anthologized in *Doorknobs and BodyPaint Fantastic Flash Fiction* (2008), and *An Eye for an Eye Makes the Whole*

World Blind, winner of the 2003 PEN Oakland Josephine Miles National Literary Award.

Judy Bebelaar | Alameda and Contra Costa Counties | Judy Bebelaar has worked as a San Francisco high school teacher with CPITS for all of her thirty-seven years of teaching, and as a poet-teacher since her retirement. Her students have won nine National Scholastic Writing Contest awards for their poetry, as well as other awards. Her poems have been published in numerous magazines, most recently *The Squaw Valley Review, Willard and Maple, The Schuylkill Valley Journal, Black Zinnias,* and *The East Bay Monthly.*

Karen Benke | Marin County | Karen Benke is the author of *Sister* (Conflu:X Press, 2004) and *RIP THE PAGE!: Creative Writing Adventures for Kids* (Shambhala, 2010). Her poems have appeared in *Ploughshares, Poetry East, Runes, Hawaii Pacific Review, Tiferet, Hungry Mind Review,* online at Poetry Daily, and elsewhere. A four-time grant recipient from the Marin Arts Council Fund for Artists, and a writing coach, she lives with her family in Mill Valley, California. Visit her at www.karenbenke.com.

Beth Beurkens | Siskiyou County | Beth Beurkens, MA, is a poet, a nonfiction writer, and a travel writer. She is the author of *By the Light of Our Dreams,* is on the faculty of the College of the Siskiyous and the Foundation for Shamanic Studies, and is a poet-teacher with CPITS. She leads the innovative writing program Writer's Heartbeat in Mount Shasta, helping writers to go deeper and express themselves more powerfully. She recently published her first collection of poetry, *Shaman's Eye.*

Duane BigEagle | Marin and Sonoma Counties | Duane BigEagle is an Osage Indian poet/writer teaching with CPITS since 1976. He won the 1993 W.A. Gerbode Award for poetry and is a traditional southern plains–style singer and dancer.

Claire Blotter | Marin County | Claire Blotter is a writer and teacher who performs poetry with movement, body percussion, and music. She has received two Marin Arts Council Individual Poet's Grants and won the 1992 and 1993 SF Performance Poetry Slams. She has taught writing at SF State University, John F. Kennedy University, Dominican University, and the College of Marin, and for the last two years, with CPITS. She has published two poetry chapbooks and received grants for poetry, theater, and video.

Jennifer Swanton Brown | Santa Clara and San Mateo Counties | Jennifer Brown (with CPITS since 2001) published her first poem in the *Palo Alto Times* when she was in fifth grade. She recently participated in Santa Clara County poet laureate Nils Peterson's project *A Family Album, Santa Clara County, 2009*. Jennifer is writing her thesis at Stanford on Eavan Boland's poetry and is a two-time recipient of a Fine Arts Commission grant from the city of Cupertino, where she lives with her family.

Christina Burress | San Diego County | Christina Burress is a new poet-teacher with CPITS, but she has been volunteering her time in the classroom for the past two years bringing poetry to fifth- through eleventh-graders. She is founder of The Del Mar Writing Project (delmarwritingproject.com), which offers workshops and camps to young and old. Her most recent work appears in the *Coe Review* and *Beasts at Bay Park Press*.

Thomas Centolella | CPITS alumnus poet-teacher | Thomas Centolella started teaching with CPITS in 1986. He is the author of three books, the latest being *Views from along the Middle Way* (Copper Canyon Press). His poems have been included in such anthologies as *Don't Tell Mama: The Penguin Book of Italian American Writing*, and *Learning by Heart: Contemporary American Poetry about School*. He has received a Lannan Literary Fellowship and the California Book Award.

Brandon Cesmat | San Diego County | Brandon Cesmat's writing appears in journals such as *Perigee, Weber: The Contemporary West*, and *Other Voices International*. His most recent books are *Light in All Directions* (poems) and *When Pigs Fall in Love* (stories). He edited *Classrooms of Poets*, which describes the CPITS program in San Diego County. He is a past president of CPITS and a founding member of Teaching Artists Organized. He teaches college in southern California.

Amanda Chiado | Santa Clara County | Amanda Chiado has proudly been a CPITS poet for five years-ish. You can find her most recent poems in *The Best New Poets 2009, Fence, The Dirty Napkin*,

Line 4, and *The Rambler*. Amanda still believes in the magic of bunnies popping out of black hats and unicorns flying over double rainbows. Forget the zombies and their mouths full of pickled skin. She will not retreat. She will not surrender.

Daryl Ngee Chinn | Humboldt County | Daryl Ngee Chinn has lived in Arcata since 1975 and teaches in Humboldt County, California, and Churchill County, Nevada. He raises money for CPITS by cooking anywhere in California and donating the proceeds. In recent years he has won the College of the Redwoods poetry prize in that college's literary magazine, *Poets and Writers*. He has also taught in Alaska, Utah, Wyoming, South Dakota, and Massachusetts. He hand-makes books, works wood, and dances Argentine tango.

Jabez W. Churchill | Sonoma and Mendocino Counties | This is Jabez Churchill's eleventh year with CPITS. It's been a good year! Two bilingual pieces just came out in *FIRST LEAVES*, Santa Rosa Junior College's art and literary journal. They were the first to be published in Spanish in the seventy-five-year history of the publication. And, this is his second consecutive year performing at the Vancouver Poetry Festival.

Veronica Cunningham | Veronica Cunningham has been a CPITS poet-teacher since 1982 and was on the Border Voices executive board for many years. Having taught K–12 extensively in schools throughout San Diego County, Veronica also taught her poetry/art integration approach in Moscow and Argentina. She is a well-known speaker at teaching conferences and has taught a variety of in-services for schools and presented at statewide and national conferences.

Arthur Dawson | Sonoma County | Arthur Dawson has taught poetry to thousands of students in Sonoma County over the last seventeen years. His work has been published in numerous local, regional, and national publications. He is also the founder and publisher of Kulupi Press, dedicated to publishing books with "a sense of place." He enjoys life in Glen Ellen with his family and has a day job as an historical ecologist. His son shares a birthday with Pablo Neruda.

Sally Doyle | San Francisco County | Sally Doyle has an MA in creative writing. For the last eight years she has worked for CPITS. She has published a chapbook, *Under the Neath* with Leave Books. Her poetry has been published in a variety of journals, such as *Chain, Lipstick Eleven,* and *five fingers review.* Most recently, her work was published in the 2009 summer issue of *Rattle.* This year she had three poems picked for public display in different San Francisco kiosks. She lives in North Beach with her husband and daughter.

Claire Drucker | Sonoma County | Claire Drucker has been a poet-teacher with CPITS for ten years and still considers this the most important work she does. In addition, Claire teaches creative writing and composition at Santa Rosa Junior College, tutors high school students, and offers classes in memoir. Her poems have been published in many journals, such as *Women Artists Datebook, Eclipse, Puerto Del Sol,* and *Diner.* Her chapbook, *Vortex,* was published in 2007. She can be reached at cdrucker_2000@yahoo.com.

Claudia Dudley | San Francisco | Claudia Dudley has worked with CPITS since 1990, and is currently poet/storyteller-in-residence with the Richmond District After School Collaborative. She has published a volume and a chapbook of poetry, and has set her own and student poems to music. She is currently bringing a book of narrative poetry with accompanying songs to completion, and hopes to make them public within the coming year.

Kathy Evans | Marin and San Francisco Counties | Kathy Evans has been a teacher with CPITS since 1982, over thirty years. She believes it is a privilege to enter through language the imagination of children of all ages. She has published three books of poetry and has taught with Writers Corps, Juvenile Hall, and Hospitality House in the Tenderloin. She won the Small Press Poetry Award for *Hunger and Sorrow,* and has been published in many journals and reviews; her most recent work was published by City Lights in *Days I Moved Through Ordinary Sound.*

Molly Fisk | CPITS alumna poet-teacher | Molly Fisk taught with CPITS for thirteen years (1994–2007), including four at Juvenile Hall. Her work has been widely published and anthologized. She's the author of the poetry collection *Listening to Winter,* and a National Endowment for the Arts fellow, and has a new CD of radio commentary called *Blow-Drying a Chicken: Observations from a Working Poet.* Molly teaches online through mollyfisk.com, poetry-bootcamp.com, and voiceofyourown.com. She lives in Nevada City, California.

PJ Flowers | Mendocino County | PJ Flowers has loved to dance and to dance words since childhood. She has worked joyfully with children and teens her whole life as a bilingual Spanish teacher of poetry, drama, creative movement, and yoga. Family, friends, nature, travel, and transcending cultural and generational divides are passions that infuse her work. PJ has performed her Movement-Poetry in the Bay Area since the 1980s and has taught for CPITS in Willits since 2006.

J. Ruth Gendler | Alameda County | J. Ruth Gendler's most recent book, *Notes on the Need for Beauty,* a book of "lyrical nonfiction," was informed by the process of teaching poetry to children and her experience as a visual artist. Her other books are *The Book of Qualities* and *Changing Light.* She began visiting classrooms to have students personify qualities in 1985 and became a CPITS poet shortly after that. Website: www.ruthgendler.com.

Terri Glass | Marin County | Terri Glass has taught with CPITS in Marin County since 1989, and now serves as the statewide program director. She has also taught poetry workshops nationally for River of Words, ChildSpirit, and the National Poetry Therapy Association. Her publications include *Unveiling the Mystical Light,* a book of poems; *Language of the Awakened Heart,* a guidebook for classroom teachers; and the award-winning poetry and music CD, *The Body of the Living Future.* Please visit www.thefoxpath.net.

Mary Lee Gowland | Madera and Fresno Counties | Mary Lee Gowland joined CPITS in 1986 and began teaching in 1991. She teaches in Madera County's "Club YES" after-school program, PTA-sponsored writing clubs, and teen workshops sponsored by the Oakhurst and Fresno County libraries. *Europe on Five Dollars a Day,* a memoir, aired on Valley Writers Read in July. It (as well as *State Beach,* which aired last year) can be heard on www.kvpr.org. Some of her poems can be heard at http://fresnopoetrycorner.podbean.com/. Website: www.maryleegowland.com.

Grace Marie Grafton | San Francisco and Alameda Counties | Grace Grafton has worked with CPITS for twenty-nine years. She has received numerous CAC residency grants for her work at Lakeshore School, San Francisco. She was named teacher of the year one year by the River of Words student poetry/art contest. Recent publications include three sonnets in *VOLT,* poems in *Edgz, Prism Review,* and *Listening Eye,* and online in *Canary, The Golden Lantern, Poetic Matrix LetteR 7, poemeleon,* and *Green Hills Literary Lantern.* She has published two books of poetry: *Zero* and *Visiting Sisters.*

Jack Grapes | CPITS alumnus poet-teacher | Jack Grapes is the editor of *ONTHEBUS,* the author of thirteen books of poetry, and has taught in over 150 schools since 1977, serving as LA coordinator for three years. He has received several NEA Fellowships in Literature and numerous grants from the California Arts Council. He wrote and starred in *Circle of Will,* a winner of theatre critic awards for Best Comedy and Best Performance. His book *Method Writing* is due for publication soon. Website: www.jackgrapes.com.

Katharine Harer | CPITS alumna poet-teacher | Katharine Harer started with CPITS in 1978. In 1979 she became office administrator and served as statewide director until 1984, when she began teaching at Skyline College. For seven years she was the director of Small Press Traffic. In 1991, she was hired full time at Skyline. She co-coordinates the Poetry and Pizza reading series in downtown San Francisco and is currently writing a nonfiction book about her travels in Chile on the trail of Pablo Neruda.

Jorge Herrera | CPITS alumnus poet-teacher.

Juan Felipe Herrera | CPITS alumnus poet-teacher | Juan Felipe's recent books are *Half of the World in Light: New and Selected Poems* (winner of the National Book Critics Circle Award in Poetry in 2009) and *187 Reasons Mexicanos Can't Cross the Border: Undocuments* (City Lights), which won the 2008 Pen National Poetry Award and the 2008 Pen/Oakland Josephine Miles National Poetry Award. His forthcoming book for young adults is *Lucky Z.* He is the

Tomás Rivera Endowed Chair in the department of creative writing at UC Riverside.

Julie Hochfeld | Humboldt County | Julie Hochfeld has been a California poet in the schools for over three years. As a three-time CAC Artists in the Schools Grant corecipient, she has taught poetry to hundreds of students. She also works as a homeschool teacher, a guest lecturer at Humboldt State University, and a continuing education teacher to classroom teachers. Her poems have appeared in *Mothering, The North Coast Journal, Toyon, College of the Redwoods Poets and Writers,* and other publications.

Jackleen Holton | San Diego County | Jackleen Holton has been a CPITS poet-teacher since 2006. Her work has appeared in *The Giant Book of Poetry, Ibbetson Street, Red River Review,* and *The Mountain Astrologer.* Her chapbook, *Devil Music,* was published by Caernarvon Press in 2005.

Maureen Hurley | Alameda, San Francisco, San Mateo, and Sonoma Counties | Maureen Hurley joined CPITS in 1979. During her AC tenure (1980s–90s), the Sonoma program grew to be the fourth largest in the state. She has won art and poetry awards: seven CAC grants, two NEA fellowships from the Community Foundation of Sonoma County, two KQED SPARK awards, and an Oakland Cultural Arts Council grant. Publication credits: *14 Hills, Transfer, Louisville Review, Santa Clara Review, Tight, Caribbean Writer, Gulf Stream.* Her Litterata and Cybernalia articles, memoirs, and poems are online at http://mohurley.blogspot.com.

Tobey Kaplan | Alameda County | Tobey Kaplan, from New York City, has been teaching children and adults in the Bay Area for over thirty years. Tobey has given creative-process workshops concerning literacy and social change. She is a poet-in-residence at community mental health centers, and an instructor of creative writing in Contra Costa County jails. She has been a Dorland Mountain Colony Fellow and an affiliate artist at the Headlands Center for the Arts, and has received a Bay Area Award (New Langton Arts, 1996). *Across the Great Divide* was published by Androgyne (1995).

Lavender Grace Kent | Mendocino County | As a student poet, Lavender Grace Kent had the pleasure of being taught by CPITS poet-teachers for six years in the Mendocino schools. She has been a poet-teacher for the past three years. Her experience with poetry has been focused on the lyrical/musical element, as she is a profes-sional musician, utilizing the glorious arena of words combined with tonalities and melody offered as gifts to her audiences in the form of songs. More information about her work can be found at www.lavendergrace.com.

Lois Klein | Santa Barbara County | Lois Klein has published two books of poetry, *Naming Water* (1998) and *A Soldier's Daughter* (Turning Point, 2008). She has been a CPITS poet-teacher for ten years, is on the faculty of the Santa Barbara Poetry Conference, organizes the monthly Favorite Poems Project, is a fellow of the South Coast Writers Project, and leads private writing groups for adults.

Luis Kong | CPITS alumnus poet-teacher | Luis Kong is a Peruvian-Chinese living in California. He has been a poet-teacher since 1986, and was the executive director of CPITS in the early '90s. Currently, he is the director of the Alameda County Library's Write to Read adult literacy program in the San Francisco Bay Area. His research on immigration, citizenship schools, race and gender, worker-owned cooperatives, racial construction among immigrants, and somatic learning in adult education has been presented at adult education research conferences, the Western Regional Research Conference, UC Berkeley, and community-based forums.

Michele Krueger | Lake County | Born in New York, Michele Krueger graduated from Lehman College, where she studied litera-ture with Billy Collins. Her work has appeared in children's antholo-gies, including *Beauty of the Beast* by Jack Prelutsky, and *Halloween Howls* by Lee Bennett Hopkins, and she has poems forthcoming in *Poem in Your Pocket for Kids*. Scholastic published a poster of her poem "RIF Day," celebrating the joy of reading for Reading Is Fundamental youth literacy programs around the country.

Melissa Kwasny | CPITS alumna poet-teacher | Melissa Kwasny lives outside of Jefferson City, Montana. She worked in the CPITS program in San Francisco from 1989 through 1996. She is the author of four books of poetry: *The Nine Senses* (forthcoming in 2011 from

Milkweed Editions), *Reading Novalis in Montana* (2009), *Thistle* (2006), and *The Archival Birds* (2000). She was the editor of *Toward the Open Field: Poets on the Art of Poetry 1800–1950* (2004).

Lucia Lemieux | Ventura County | Lucia Lemieux is a poet and credentialed K–12 teacher from Ventura County, where she served as the area coordinator for the last ten years. She joined CPITS in 1997, and edited the 2008 CPITS anthology, *On the Other Side of Tomorrow*. Lucia has published several poems and books, holds an MFA from the American Film Institute, and is the librarian for Newbury Park High School. She continues to teach poetry in the juvenile justice system.

Daniel Zev Levinson | Humboldt County | Dan Zev Levinson teaches poetry to a thousand students each year. He has taught at over fifty sites with CPITS since 1998. He has taught at Humboldt State University, College of the Redwoods, and the Redwood Coast Writers' Center, and is a teacher-consultant for the Redwood Writing Project. Being a freelance editor and writing consultant — www.ZevLev.com — Dan has acted as a contributing editor to various publications. His poems and other writings have appeared in many journals and anthologies.

Karen Lewis | Mendocino County | Karen Lewis began teaching poetry in 1995 and loves to awaken student imagination using poetry across the curriculum. Her poems, short fiction, and essays have appeared in publications for young readers and also in literary journals including *Iron Horse, Drumvoices,* and *Hip Mama.* Karen teaches as an adjunct at Mendocino College, is on the board of the Mendocino Coast Writers Conference, and has been awarded three California Arts Council/AIS grants.

Karen Llagas | San Francisco and San Mateo Counties | Karen Llagas's poems have appeared recently or are forthcoming in *Crab Orchard Review, {m}aganda magazine, Broadsided Press,* and in the anthologies *Field of Mirrors* (PAWA, 2008) and *Poems of the San Francisco Bay Area Watershed* (Sixteen Rivers Press, 2010). Some of her poems received a Dorothy Sargent Rosenberg Poetry Prize in 2007. Karen lives in San Francisco and works as a Tagalog interpreter and instructor. She has been with CPITS since 2007.

Dana Teen Lomax | Marin County | Dana Teen Lomax is the author of *Disclosure* (Black Radish, 2009), *Curren¢y* (Palm Press, 2006), and *Room* (a+bend press, 1999), and the coeditor of *Letters to Poets: Conversations about Poetics, Politics, and Community* (Saturnalia Books, 2008). She is currently editing *Kindergarde: Avant-Garde Poems, Plays, & Stories for Children* and teaching at San Francisco State University, San Francisco School of the Arts, and Marin Juvenile Hall. She lives in San Quentin with her awesome daughter and fabulous husband.

Perie Longo | Santa Barbara | Perie Longo has been a CPITS teacher for twenty-six years, and an area coordinator for twenty-one. She was the Santa Barbara poet laureate from 2007–09. She has published three books, her latest being *With Nothing behind but Sky: a journey through grief* (2006). Her work has appeared in over fifty journals. On the staff of the Santa Barbara Writers Conference since 1984, she also leads a three-day summer poetry workshop and, as a psychotherapist, uses poetry for healing.

Alison Luterman | CPITS alumna poet-teacher | Alison Luterman's first book is *The Largest Possible Life*, published by Cleveland State University Press. Her second book is *See How We Almost Fly*, published by Pearl Editions. She also writes essays and plays, and performs spoken-word improvisation with the performance troupe Wing It!

Teresa McNeil MacLean | Madera and Santa Barbara Counties | Santa Ynez artist /musician/writer Teresa McNeil MacLean (www.teresamcneilmaclean.com) has taught poetry classes in elementary school classrooms in and around the Santa Ynez Valley since 1986; she has been a CPITS member for over ten years. Each of her workshops culminates in a public reading at a local coffeehouse. Her writing reflects the natural magic of the places she paints, often segueing from free verse to song lyrics.

devorah major | San Francisco, Marin, and Alameda Counties | devorah major has spent thirty plus years with CPITS in many capacities, including executive director. She served as San Francisco's third poet laureate from 2002–05. She is a poet, spoken word performer, novelist, short story writer, and arts educator and activist. Recent books include *where river meets ocean* and *Brown Glass Windows*. Word Temple Press released a fine-press limited-edition chapbook, *black bleeds into green*, in 2009. www.redroom.com/authors/devorah-major.

Seretta Martin | San Diego County | Seretta Martin is the San Diego author of *Foreign Dust Familiar Rain*, an *Atlanta Review* finalist, a Barnes & Noble poetry host, and a Border Voices Poetry Project poet-teacher coordinator/web designer. She is also an SDPA regional editor. Her poems have appeared in *Margie, Oberon, Oasis, Poppyseed Kilache, A Year in Ink, The California Quarterly, The Best of Border Voices*, and several anthologies, international newspapers, and websites. A book review is forthcoming on *Web Del Sol*. Website: web.mac.com/serettamartin.

Yvonne Mason | Los Angeles and Orange Counties | Yvonne Mason has been a food and dining editor since 1975, and a member of the Southern California Restaurant Writers since 1990. She is a member of the International Food Wine & Travel Writers and contributes to many publications. A poet/artist, she has been a professional poet-teacher with CPITS since 1985, and was the South Coast area coordinator for many years. She has been a recipient of NEA and CAC grants for her poems/drawings and is an award-winning photographer.

Michael McLaughlin | San Luis Obispo, Santa Barbara, and Monterey Counties | Originally from San Francisco, Michael McLaughlin has worked as a poet-teacher with CPITS for nineteen years; as an artist-in-residence at Atascadero State Hospital, a maximum security forensic facility; and as a contract artist with the California Department of Corrections. A graduate of USC's Master of Professional Writing program, he has written one novel and three books of poetry. He is currently completing his second novel, *Gang of One*, and served as the poet laureate of San Luis Obispo, California, in 2003.

MaryLee McNeal | Santa Clara | MaryLee McNeal began teaching with CPITS in 1993. Her poems have been published in various magazines and anthologies. Her novel won the Clark Award at San Francisco State University, and her short stories, published in the *Bellevue Literary Review* and other magazines, have been nominated for Pushcart and Henfield awards. She leads a weekly poetry workshop at Hope House, a Redwood City residential drug and alcohol recovery program.

Alexa Mergen | Sacramento County | Alexa Mergen joined CPITS in 2004 and serves as the Sacramento area coordinator. She has worked with thousands of students of all ages in classrooms and community settings as a teacher, teacher mentor, and teaching artist, and is active in integrating poetry and children's literature with humane and environmental education. Her chapbook, *We Have Trees*, combines typography, prose, and poetry with a travel memoir. E-mail her at alexamergen@yahoo.com.

Phyllis Meshulam | Sonoma County | Phyllis Meshulam celebrates ten years with CPITS this year. Letters to the editor are still her most widely circulated writings. Recent poetry publications credits are from *Out of Line* journal and *The Haight Ashbury Literary Journal*. Her poem, "Weaving Peace," was set by composer Diane Benjamin as the finale of an original choral piece commissioned by the Denver Women's Chorus. Phyllis has just finished editing a one-hundred-page anthology of student work from Napa State Hospital.

Tureeda 'ToRead ah' Mikell, (c) | Alameda County | Tureeda has been a BAWP fellow since 1996, a CPITS instructor since 1990, and has published over sixty anthologies of students' work. She loves to witness the excitement students release on paper while she is teaching poetry in the classroom. Her most recent publication, *Tembu Tupu*, is an anthology released in Japan 2009 by Kinokuniya, and in Chicago via Emory University; contributors include Rita Dove, Nikki Giovanni, June Jordan, Maya Angelou, Audre Lorde, and others.

Florencia Milito | San Francisco County | Born in Argentina, Florencia Milito has lived in the United States since she was nine. Her work has appeared in as *Sniper Logic*, *ZYZZYVA*, *27 Hours* (Kearny Street Press), *ZNET en Español*, and the *Indiana Review*. She was a semifinalist for the 2003 Nation/Discovery Poetry Prize, a finalist in the 2007 California Writers Exchange contest, and a recipient of a 2007 Hedgebrook Foundation residency. She has been with CPITS since 2008.

Joseph D. Milosch | San Diego | Joe Milosch graduated in 1995 with an MFA from San Diego State University. His first book, *The Lost Pilgrimage Poems*, was published by Poetic Matrix. His poems "Among Men" and "Letters from Paul" were nominated for the Pushcart Prize. He received an honorable mention for his poetry in the Chapel Jazz Poetry Contest in the spring of 1999. He received an Excellence in Literature award from MiraCosta College.

minerva | CPITS alumna poet-teacher | minerva (Gail N. Hawkins) has an MA from the University of Massachusetts and was a poet-in-residence for the Maryland Arts Council before becoming a poet-teacher in California. She is a writer for the entertainment industry, a performer, and the leader of two jazz bands. Her poetry has been frequently published.

Blake More | Mendocino and Sonoma Counties | A CPITS poet-teacher since 2000, Blake More currently serves as the Mendocino County area coordinator and as the CPITS webstress. Blake's creative work spans the spectrum from poetry, fiction, and performance pieces to theatrical costumes, mixed media, video, and poetry art cars. Her newest book, *godmeat,* is a collection of poetry, prose, color artwork, and a DVD compilation of poem movies (available at www.godmeat.com). To explore Blake's creative world, visit www.snakelyone.com.

Jill Moses | San Diego | Jill Moses earned her MFA in creative writing from the University of Oregon, where she received the graduate award in poetry and served as assistant poetry editor of the *Northwest Review.* Current publications include the *Magee Park Poetry Anthology, The CPITS Newsletter,* and the *San Diego Poetry Annual.* She has been affiliated with CPITS for nine years, serves on the board of CPITS, and teaches middle school humanites at Rancho Encinitas Academy.

Johnnierenee Nelson | San Diego | Johnnierenee Nelson has written five books of Kwanzaa poetry, her latest being *Classic Kwanzaa Poems: New and Selected.* She received Michigan State University's Creative Writing Award for Best Collection of Poetry for her volume *21 Years toward Becoming a Black Woman,* and has been a member of CPITS for seventeen years. She is currently completing a children's book titled *If I Were a Blackberry*. She loves world travel and dance.

Gail Newman | San Francisco | Gail Newman was born in Germany, raised in Los Angeles, and lives in San Francisco, and has worked for CPITS for over thirty years. Gail is a museum educator at the Contemporary Jewish Museum in San Francisco. Her students' poems have been featured on ArtSpark (television) and in Houghton Mifflin's English textbooks. She is the editor of *C is for California,* an alphabet book of poems written by children.

Richard Newsham | Ventura County | A poet-teacher locally for over twenty years, Richard Newsham was most recently published in *Askew* and *Ventura Life*. He studied at Warwick and Oxford Universities; has a BA in English/classics from Duke University; and did graduate work at the University of Toronto, the Sorbonne, and Yale University in comparative literature and Renaissance art history.

Gwynn O'Gara | Sonoma County | Gwynn O'Gara has worked with CPITS for twenty years and is the author of *Snake Woman Poems* (Beatitude Press), *Fixer-Upper* (dpress), and *Winter at Green Haven* (Word Temple Press). Recent and upcoming publications include *Beatitude's 50th Anniversary Anthology, The Evansville Review, CALYX, Sage Woman,* and *descant.*

Chris Olander | Nevada, Placer, Sacramento, and Mendocino Counties | Chris Olander, poet and bio-educator with CPITS since 1984, blends performance techniques with spoken word to create an Action Art Poetry: relative-time phrasing of musical images to dramatize experiences; a poetics arising from oral and bardic traditions. "I am a sound poet exploring various meanings of words, ideas, and phrasings arranged in sound and rhythm patterns." Chris's student, Roshawnda Bettencourt, whose poem is included in this anthology, won the California State Poetry Out Loud Championship in April, 2008.

Eva Poole-Gilson | Inyo and Mono Counties | Eva Poole-Gilson has taught poetry for thirty years and published numerous poems and essays in journals — often in *The Mammoth Monthly, The Inyo Register,* and *The Mammoth Times*. She has organized eighteen annual three-day poetry conferences for third–twelfth-graders in

Inyo/Mono Counties, taught over sixty CPITS poets, and led final conference readings and celebrations. Her two books are *Love Letter from a Poet to the High Sierra* and *Little Star Sleeping*, available from PegasusArtBooksCollectibles.com or bkebkb@hotmail.com.

Scott Reid | Sonoma County | Scott Reid, MA, presents poetry writing classes for children in Sonoma County with CPITS. His poems have appeared in *Blue Unicorn, The Berkeley Poetry Review, Melic Review, Sow's Ear,* and *The Dickens,* and he has received writing fellowships from the Squaw Valley Writers' Conference, the Napa Valley Writers' Conference, and the Bread Loaf Writers' Conference. As a presenter of poetry for adults since 1989, he has taught many classes in poetry at the Albany Adult School in Albany, California.

Michele Rivers | Marin County | Michele Rivers is an English Renaissance woman: a writer, artist, photographer, and teacher. She is an active CPITS teacher and has written several books, including *Time for Tea: Tea and Conversations with Thirteen English Women.* She is currently writing *Venus's Nipple: Sensual Short Stories Featuring Italian Locations.* Michele is the creator of the Gift of Love Poetry program, a nonprofit that provides complimentary poetry CDs to people diagnosed with cancer: www.giftoflovepoetry.com.

Shelley Savren | Ventura County | Shelley Savren's book, *The Common Fire,* was published by Red Hen Press (2004). Her poems appear in *Solo* and *Prairie Schooner.* Shelley has received nine CAC grants, two NEA regional grants, and five fellowships from the city of Ventura. She has taught poetry workshops at a men's prison and juvenile detention centers, to emotionally disturbed adolescents, and at every grade through CPITS for over three decades. She lives in Ventura and is a full-time English professor at Oxnard College.

Prartho Sereno | Marin County | Prartho Sereno is the author/illustrator of the poetry collection *Causing a Stir: The Secret Lives and Loves of Kitchen Utensils,* winner of a 2008 IPPY award. Her other publications include *Call from Paris* (2007 Word Works Washington Prize) and *Everyday Miracles* (essays). She received a Radio Disney Super Teacher Award for her ten years with CPITS. Anything she gets right in her poems she owes to her students, especially the second-graders.

Mara Sheade | Alameda and Santa Clara Counties | Mara

Sheade has been a poet-teacher for over ten years. She introduced the CPITS program to students in Fremont, Newark, and Milpitas over five years ago. Her poems have appeared in *The Paterson Literary Review, Voices of the Grieving Heart,* and the *Journal of Poetry Therapy,* as well as in several anthologies.

Susan Herron Sibbet | San Francisco County | Susan Herron Sibbet has been poet-in-residence with CPITS throughout the Bay Area for twenty-five years. With her MA in creative writing from San Francisco State University, Susan was a Bunting Fellow at the Radcliffe Institute and an affiliate artist with the Headlands Center for the Arts. She helped found Sixteen Rivers Press, a Bay Area poetry collective. *No Easy Light,* her third book of poems, was published by Sixteen Rivers Press in 2004.

Celia Sigmon | San Diego County | Celia Sigmon graduated Phi Kappa Phi, earning a MFA in creative writing, from San Diego State University, where she teaches composition in the Department of Rhetoric and Writing Skills. She has been a Border Voices poet for fifteen years and has been actively involved in all aspects of the program: as an anthology judge, as a volunteer at the fair, as the area coordinator for the Border Voices poet-teachers and CPITS, and as a board member.

Eleni Sikelianos | CPITS alumna poet-teacher | Eleni Sikelianos taught with CPITS from 1991–93. She is now an associate professor at the University of Denver, where she has started a writers-in-the-schools training for her students. Her books include a memoir (*The Book of Jon,* City Lights) and six volumes of poetry; the most recent title is *Body Clock.* She has been the happy recipient of a National Endowment for the Arts Award, a Fulbright Fellowship, and awards from The National Poetry Series, the New York Foundation for the Arts, and the Gertrude Stein Award for Innovative American Writing.

giovanni singleton | Marin County | Poet giovanni singleton is the founding editor of *nocturnes (re)view,* a journal dedicated to work of the African Diaspora and other contested spaces. Her work has appeared in *Fence, Callaloo,* and *Alehouse.* She has taught poetry at the de Young Museum, the Oakland Museum, and Saint Mary's

College in Moraga, California. She currently teaches with CPITS in the San Francisco Bay Area.

Gary Soto | Gary Soto is a prolific author of books for children, young adults, and adults. His best-known titles include *Chato's Kitchen, Too Many Tamales, Baseball in April, Buried Onions,* and *New and Selected Poems.* He was recognized by NBC news for his advocacy for reading as Person of the Week. The Gary Soto Literary Museum will open in fall 2010 at Fresno City College, where he first became acquainted with poetry.

Will Staple | Nevada County | Will Staple lives alone in a cabin in the Sierra. He meets with friends three afternoons a week for saunas and conversation. Each spring he visits the Grand Canyon for a week of off-trail backpacking. He teaches poetry in the schools twelve weeks a year, where he awards poetic licenses to students who give him goosebumps when they read their poems aloud. Every other year he tours Europe, where he gives readings and visits friends.

Susan Terence | San Francisco County | Susan Terence, a San Francisco CPITS poet-teacher for over twenty years, has won several writing awards and been published widely. She has a BA in English Ed. from the University of Arizona, an MA in inter-arts education, and an MFA in creative writing from San Francisco State. She has been a writer- and performing-artist-in-residence throughout the country, and has been named Creative Writing Teacher of the year by the SF Unified School District.

Marissa Bell Toffoli | Alameda and Contra Costa Counties | After years of independently visiting classrooms to teach poetry, Marissa Toffoli joined CPITS as a poet-teacher in 2009. She works as an editor and writer. Marissa earned an MFA in creative writing from California College of the Arts. Her poems have been published in many print and online journals, most recently *Train Tracts* and *RHINO.* For more information, visit her Google profile: http://www.google.com/profiles/102891497126491313694.

Emmanuel Williams | San Mateo County | Emmanuel Williams is a qualified teacher with forty-plus years of international experience. His writing has been featured on BBC and NPR, and he has been published in the following magazines: *Pennwood Review, Staple,*

Toyan, Penumbra, Resurgence, Sacred Fire, Snowy Egret, and *The Countryman.* His books are *Living in Light* (Phillips Publications), and *Man Without Bones* (Robert R. Reed). He has published riddle cards with Pomegranate, and *A–Z of Imaginary Fish* through Lulu. He is working on interactive riddle website and a novel.

Toni Wynn | CPITS alumna poet-teacher | San Luis Obispo | Toni Wynn loved the five years (1992–97) that she worked as a poet-teacher with CPITS. Michael McLaughlin drafted her; he assured her that she was right for the organization. She still can't get enough of doing creative writing residencies and workshops with children! She is now an education director and artist/faculty with Young Audiences of Virginia. Her most recent book is *Ground,* a letterpress, book-art limited edition published by Shakespeare Press Museum in San Luis Obispo, available at etsy.com.

Pamela Raphael Yezbick | Sonoma County | Pamela Yezbick has been a poet-teacher with CPITS since 1980. She was the humane educator for the Humane Society of Sonoma County for nine years. During this time, she wrote *Teaching Compassion,* a narrative replete with children's poems and drawings that explains to educators and parents how to teach respect, responsibility, and compassion to children through their remarkable relationships with animals. In 1992, Pamela was chosen as the Humane Educator of the Year.

RESOURCES

SO YOU WANT TO BE PUBLISHED?

Before you send any work in:

- Check the writers' guidelines, which are usually either on the website or inside the magazine.
- Follow all the guidelines carefully.
- Pay attention to word count, themes, or other specifics that might be requested. For example, type your name and the page number on each page, unless requested not to — sometimes contests want "blind" manuscripts with a separate cover sheet with your information.
- Be familiar with the venue where you are sending you work.
- Adhere strictly to any deadlines.
- Send your best work.
- Have a teacher, friend, or parent check your manuscript for typos first.
- Use white paper, 8 1/2 x 11 inches, and black ink with a serif font like Times Roman / 12 pt.
- Include a brief cover letter.
- Include a SASE (self-addressed stamped envelope) so that the publisher can reply to your submission.
- Keep a copy of the work that you submit and the date that you submitted it.

At some point, sooner or later, you will be rejected. Keep sending out work, and keep making work. Do not let one person's opinion discourage you. When your work is published, you will receive a copy of the issue, and possibly a payment.

Keep copies of all your published work, and don't forget to share it with those who love you.

Remember: Persistence is key!

SO YOUR WRITING NEEDS A HOME?

Creative Kids magazine publishes cartoons, songs, stories between 500 and 1,200 words, puzzles, photographs, artwork, games, editorials, poetry, and plays, as well as any other creative work that can fit in the pages of the magazine by students (ages 8–16). An archive of resources for teaching and parenting gifted children. www.prufrock.com.

Hanging Loose magazine has published high school writers in every issue, and they have put together several anthologies of high school writing: Hanging Loose Press, 231 Wyckoff St., Brooklyn, NY 11217. www.hangingloosepress.com.

Imagine: A magazine for students 12–18, publishes stories, poems, essays, and book reviews: Editor, CTY/Imagine, Johns Hopkins University, 3400 N. Charles St., Baltimore, MD 21218. Or visit them on the web at www.jhu.edu/gifted/imagine/guidelines. Also offers a variety of academic opportunities.

Merlyn's Pen: An annual publication of essays, stories, and poems by students in grades 6–12. Check it out at www.merlynspen.com. A large archive of resources for writers and teachers.

New Moon: The Magazine for Girls and Their Dreams, for girls age 8–14. New Moon, 34 East Superior St, No. 200, Duluth, MN 55802. www.newmoon.org.

River of Words sponsors an annual poetry and art contest for students. www.riverofwords.org.

Skipping Stones features a multicultural, international perspective. Poetry, personal-experience essays, and short stories: Skipping Stones, P.O. Box 3939, Eugene, OR 97403. www.skippingstones.org.

Stone Soup: Publishes poems and stories by kids through age 13. www.stonesoup.com.

Scholastic magazine has an annual competition for writers, photographers, and artists. For grades 7–12. The website has complete information on entries and examples of past award winners. www.artandwriting.org.

Teen Ink publishes poetry and short prose online and in print. Read a sample before submitting your work. Information about workshops, college programs and related writer resources. www.teenink.com.

Waging Peace. A wealth of peace resources, including poetry and essay contests. www.wagingpeace.org.

Writing Magazine, Weekly Reader, 200 First Stamford Place, Stamford, CT 06912. For grades 6–10. Editor Sandhya Nankani says "We are always looking to publish student writing." E-mail her at snankani@weeklyreader.com for guidelines.

SO YOU NEED RESOURCES?

Academy of American Poets. Find a poet, find a poem. www.poets.org.

Center for the Art of Translation promotes literature and translation. Home of Poetry Inside Out, a bilingual school-based program. Anthologies available. www.catranslation.org.

California Poets in the Schools, 1333 Balboa Street, San Francisco, CA 94118. (415) 221-4201. www.cpits.org. Places professional writers in classrooms throughout California.

Carnegie Library. Resources and literature for children and teens. www.clpgh.org.

InnerSpark: A summer program for students in 8th–12th grade passionate about music, creative writing, dance, film, visual art, animation, or theatre. Find their website at www.csssa.org.

New York Public Library. Literary resources for students, writers & teachers. www.nypl.org.

Oyate, 2702 Matthews St., Berkeley, CA 94702. Native American Studies. Oyate is the Dakota name for "people." www.oyate.org.

Poetry Foundation: Committed to bringing poetry to everyone. A wonderful site to find a poem or to learn about new forms like poetry-comics. www. poetryfoundation.org.

Poetry Out Loud: Sponsored by the National Endowment for the Arts, this program offers instruction to high school students on the art of recitation and poetry performance. Great poems archived on site. www. poetryoutloud.org.

Poets & Writers is published bimonthly with interviews, publication opportunities, and links to other literary sites. www.pw.org.

San Francisco State University Poetry Archives: A wide range of video, audio, and written work by living and historic poets. A diverse range of styles and voices. www.sfsu. edu/~poetry.

Teachers & Writers Collaborative, 5 Union Square West, NYC 10003-3306. Publishes a catalog of writing tools and offers a comprehensive website with many literary links. www. twc.org.

Teaching Tolerance: Lesson plans, and posters free to educators and students. www.tolerance.org.

WriteGirl provides mentoring, creative writing workshops, and performance and publication opportunities for teen girls in the Los Angeles region. Find them at www.writegirl.org.

Writers Corps, a project of the SF Arts Commission, reaches out to youth ages 6–14 in a variety of neighborhood and school centers. www.writerscorps-sf.org.

Youth Speaks. Written and spoken word in the SF Bay Area. www.youthspeaks.org.

826 Valencia Street Project, in San Francisco's Mission District, offers writing programs for all age groups. Includes poetry, science fiction, experimental writing, bookmaking, and tutoring. They welcome English-language learners. Check it out at www.826valencia.org. In Los Angeles, find program details at www.826la.org.

SO YOU NEED INSPIRATION?

Best of 2008

Poems

Alarcón, Francisco X. *Animal Poems of the Iguazú / Animalario del Iguazú.* San Francisco, CA: Children's Book Press. Animal spirits; Spanish/English; vivid, energetic art.

Ashman, Linda. *Stella, Unleashed.* New York: Sterling. Fun rescue-dog poems from the dog's point of view.

Beck, Carolyn. *Buttercup's Lovely Day.* Custer, WA: Orca Books. A day in the life of a contented cow, lyrical illustrations.

Giovanni, Nikki, ed. *Hip Hop Speaks to Children.* Illinois: Sourcebooks. A broad range of African American voices, audio CD.

Greenberg, Jan. *Side by Side: New Poems Inspired by Art from Around the World.* New York: Abrams. (Multilingual)

Holbrook, Sara and Wolf, Allan. *More Than Friends; Poems from Him and Her.* Honesdale, PA: Wordsong/Boyds Mills Press. Teen boy and girl perspectives, fun sidebars on poetic form and experimentation.

Hopkins, Lee Bennett. *America at War.* New York: McElderry. Poets on war, historical perspective, mural-like art.

Lombardo, Tom, ed. *After Shocks: The Poetry of Recovery for Life-Shattering Events.* Poets on topics like loss, stress, war and death.

Lawson, Jonarno. ***Black Stars in a White Night Sky.*** Honesdale, PA: Boyds Mills/Wordsong. Poems from silly to serious, playful to absurd, poignant to wry.

Lewis, J. Patrick and Graves, Keith. ***The World's Greatest: Poems.*** San Francisco: Chronicle Books. Fun facts and factoids become the focus of clever poems in varied formats.

Nye, Naomi Shihab. ***Honeybee.*** New York: Greenwillow. Poem gems, vignettes, and observations.

Rex, Adam. ***Frankenstein Takes the Cake.*** New York: Harcourt. Hysterical riffs on monsters in poems, parodies, art.

Siddall, Stephen and Ward, Mary, eds. ***The Truth about Love: A Collection of Writing on Love Through the Ages.*** New York: Cambridge University Press. All kinds of love, all kinds of voices.

Soto, Gary. ***Partly Cloudy: Poems of Love and Longing.*** Boston: Houghton Mifflin Harcourt. Young love poems, with crossover character connections.

Wheeler, Lesley. ***Voicing American Poetry: Sound and Performance from the 1920s to the Present.*** New York: Cornell Press. Historical voice and performance from poets such as Langston Hughes.

Poetry by Kids

Franco, Betsy, ed. ***Falling Hard: 100 Love Poems by Teenagers.*** Cambridge, MA: Candlewick. Teen perspectives, broad and moving.

Michael, Pamela, ed. ***River of Words.*** Minneapolis, MN: Milkweed. Eco-themed poems by kids, international writing contest, inspiring and challenging.

Verse Novels

Engle, Margarita. ***The Surrender Tree.*** New York: Holt. Cuban history, true story, heroic woman, multiple viewpoints.

Frost, Helen. ***Diamond Willow.*** New York: Farrar, Straus &

Giroux. Alaskan setting, girl growing up, mystical ancestors, great dogs, new form.

Herrick, Steven. *Naked Bunyip Dancing.* Honesdale, PA: Boyds Mills/Wordsong. Classroom characters, inspiring teacher, hilarious talent show.

Nelson, Marilyn. *The Freedom Business.* Asheville, NC: Front Street. Nonfiction slave narrative, evocative art.

Smith, Hope Anita. *Keeping the Night Watch.* New York: Henry Holt. Absent father returns, son rebels, family dynamics shift.

Weatherford, Carole Boston. *Becoming Billie Holiday.* Honesdale, PA: Wordsong/Boyds Mills Press. Poems channel music and music history, biography through poetry.

Zimmer, Tracie Vaughn. *42 Miles.* New York: Clarion. Divorce and division, dual identities, girl growing up, quirky art.

Nonfiction About Poetry

Bryant, Jen. *A River of Words: The Story of William Carlos Williams.* New York: Eerdmans Books for Young Readers. Biographical picture book, poetic illustrations.

Lawson, JonArno. *Inside Out: Children's Poets Discuss Their Work.* London: Walker. Poems plus creation commentary from two dozen international poets.

Prelutsky, Jack. *Pizza, Pigs, and Poetry; How to Write a Poem.* New York: Greenwillow. How-to, helpful tips, behind the scenes glimpses, hilarious and outrageous.

Steinman, Lisa M. *Invitation to Poetry: The Pleasures of Studying Poetry and Poetics (How to Study Literature).* Blackwell Publishing: Massachusetts. A range of poems and styles, some theory and examination.

CPITS poet-teachers and friends at the "Full Circle" Symposium in Santa Barbara, August 28–30, 2009.

CPITS POET-TEACHERS 2008–09

ALAMEDA COUNTY
Judy Bebelaar, J. Ruth Gendler, Grace Grafton, Maureen Hurley, Tobey Kaplan, Alison Luterman, Tureeda Mikell, Kristin Palm, Alison Seevak, Mara Sheade, Elijah Smith, Marissa Bell Toffoli

BUTTE & TEHAMA COUNTIES
Heather Altfeld

HUMBOLDT COUNTY
Daryl Chinn, Julie Hochfeld, Daniel Zev Levinson

INYO COUNTY
Eva Poole-Gilson

LAKE COUNTY
Michele Krueger

LOS ANGELES COUNTY
Fernando Castro, David Del Bourgo, Kirsten Ogden

MADERA COUNTY
Mary Lee Gowland, L. Anne Molin

MARIN COUNTY
Lea Aschkenas, Karen Benke, Duane BigEagle, Brandon Bishop, Claire Blotter, Sasha Eakle, Kathy Evans, Terri Glass, Dana Lomax, Michele Rivers, Prartho Sereno, giovanni singleton

MENDOCINO COUNTY
Jabez W. Churchill, PJ Flowers, Lavender Grace Kent, Karen Lewis, Ilona Starr Marcello, Blake More, Chris Olander, Dan Roberts

NEVADA, PLACER, & SIERRA COUNTIES
Chris Olander, Will Staple

SACRAMENTO COUNTY
Jo Ann M. Anglin, Chris Olander, Alexa Mergen

SAN DIEGO COUNTY
Christina Burress, Brandon Cesmat, Veronica Cunningham, Glory Foster, Jackleen Holton, Seretta Martin, Joseph Milosch, Jill Moses, Johnnierenee Nelson, Celia Sigmon

SAN FRANCISCO COUNTY
Brandon Bishop, Jim Cartwright, Sally Doyle, Claudia Dudley, Kathy Evans, Karen Llagas, devorah major, Florencia Milito, D. Scot Miller, Gail Newman, Kristin Palm, Susan Sibbet, Susan Terence

SAN LUIS OBISPO COUNTY
Michael McLaughlin

SAN MATEO COUNTY
Cathy Barber, Karen Llagas, MaryLee McNeal, Emmanuel Williams

SANTA BARBARA COUNTY
Lois Klein, Christine Kravetz, Perie Longo, Teresa McNeil MacLean, Chryss Yost

SANTA CLARA COUNTY
Jennifer Swanton Brown, Amanda Chiado, MaryLee McNeal

ABOUT US

We help students throughout California to recognize and celebrate their own creativity, intuition, and intellectual curiosity through the creative writing process. Our multicultural community of poet-teachers bring their experience and love for their craft into the classroom every school day.

California Poets in the Schools is the largest artist-in-residence program in the nation. We have been bringing our program to schools since 1964. Though we are not part of any one school district, we teach in public and private schools, juvenile halls, and hospital programs, and send over one hundred poets into classrooms throughout California.

Our poet-teachers are professional, published writers who are trained in the art of teaching poetry to children. They are from diverse cultural and ethnic heritages and serve as living models of commitment to imaginative language and creativity.

We endeavor to make creative writing an integral part of the education of young people. We encourage young people to recognize, examine, and value culture, imagination, perception, and creativity, and help them foster an appreciation for self-expression. We also share and affirm the cultural diversity of California by bringing poets and artists of color into the classroom and using multicultural materials in our lessons.

We hope you enjoy this anthology of our poet-teachers' and students' work. Please consider supporting California Poets in the Schools in any amount by visiting us on the web at www. cpits.org. and clicking the "donate now" button, or by contacting us at:

California Poets in the Schools
1333 Balboa Street, #3
San Francisco, CA 94118
(415) 221-4201
www.cpits.org • info@cpits.org